my shouting, shattered, whispering voice

Also by Patrice Vecchione

my
SHOUTING,
shattered,
whispering

**A Guide to
Writing Poetry
& Speaking
Your Truth**

PATRICE
VECCHIONE

NEW YORK • OAKLAND • LONDON

A SEVEN STORIES PRESS FIRST EDITION

Seven Stories Press 140 Watts Street
New York, NY 10013
www.sevenstories.com

Library of Congress Cataloging-in-Publication Data

NAMES: Vecchione, Patrice, author.
TITLE: My shouting, shattered, whispering voice : a guide to writing
poetry and speaking your truth / Patrice Vecchione.
IDENTIFIERS: LCCN 2019030537 | ISBN 9781609809850
(paperback) | ISBN 9781609809867 (ebk)
SUBJECTS: LCSH: Poetry—Authorship—Study and teaching.
CLASSIFICATION: LCC PN1059.A9 V383 2020 | DDC 808.1—dc23
LC record available at https://lccn.loc.gov/2019030537

Printed in the USA.

9 8 7 6 5 4 3 2 1

For a girl I knew once and for a long time
and in memory of my mother, Peggy Vecchione,
for the gifts of poetry and courage

The necessity of poetry has to be stated over and over . . .
to those who have reason to fear its power,
or those who still believe
that language is "only" words.
—ADRIENNE RICH

Contents

PART II

"If One Part Were Touched, the Whole Would Tremble":
Writing Poetry from the Inside Out

PART III

Who Said You Couldn't Say That?: Twenty-Five Poetry-Writing Suggestions in Twenty-One Short Chapters

PART IV

"How Possible Might the Impossible Be?":
Getting Your Poetry Out There

PART V

Where to Go from Here: Poetry Resources

xi

INTRODUCTION
A Chewed-Up Pencil in the Back Pocket
of an Old Pair of Jeans

Once upon a time a girl lost her voice. She had been
treated cruelly, and for years, she said not a yes or a no.
What she couldn't say out loud—the unspeakable and the
everyday things—she turned into poems, and that led
her later to reclaim her voice, anew, aloud.

Once upon another time a boy kept a journal that he
filled with his life's challenges and triumphs. When his
father found the notebook he read it, and in front of the
boy, he set a match to his son's words. That would have
kept many from writing again. This young man bought a
new notebook, wrote a new poem, and after memorizing
it, tore out the page and set a match to it himself. At the
top of the next page he wrote the first word of his new
poem. If his father were to read it, there would be noth-
ing to anger him. This notebook with the mostly missing
words later became the young poet's first book. Such was
the determination of the poet within him.

Our lives are made of stories and poems, from the tini-
est incidents to the biggest—early childhood experiences
like icing your first cake to more recent ones like a first
crush. There's hitting your first home run, the private
embarrassment of cheating on a test and not getting
caught, a #MeToo moment.

Writing poems is a way to uncover what most needs
to be uncovered—to loosen the tongue in solitude, to

make connections that can't be made in conversation. Poems are made of questions more than answers. They can withstand sudden shifts of direction, may be full of contradictions. Poems don't shy away from incomplete sentences. A poem of no more than three lines can defy darkness or change the wind's direction. The poet Kwame Dawes said, "Poetry offers us the capacity to carry in us and express the contradictory impulses that make us human."

Once upon another time there was a kid who was overwhelmed by her life. She needed a way to reckon with her confusions, those knotted and gooey ones that pressed against her. Her father's daily shouting in Italian and English made his eyes spin, and when he called her an idiot, she wanted to disappear. She was embarrassed by the slurred speech of her mother's drunken public outbursts. At school she felt out of place, as though the oddities of her home life were visible. In front of most others she was quiet. But inside her head loud bees were swarming.

One morning during her first year of high school, wearing the brown felt hat with the beaded sunburst on the front (the hat she wore even to bed), her long hair falling down the length of her back, she walked out of class, giving no reason. Behind the music building, late morning winter sun leaned warm against the wall and she sat down. Someone was playing drums inside a classroom. But the girl was listening to something else, something within her, and it was persistent.

Pulling out a small notebook and a chewed-up pencil from the back pocket of her jeans, the girl began to write. Unlike the dread and drudgery that came with classroom writing, this was nearly effortless. It was as if the poem were writing her. She read it once to herself. Satisfied, she returned to class.

That girl was me. For a long time, my poems stayed hidden in notebooks. I wrote to make something out of what scared me, to separate myself from the crazy instability of my home life and the sense of not fitting in at school. To say how it felt, I wrote to save my life. Not for a long time did I have an inkling that within me there were books to be written, that I could become a writer.

That was lifetimes ago, really. That books have my name on the spine continues to amaze and delight me. When the first copy of a new one arrives in the mail, I'm glad you can't see me because I dance around the house, holding the book in my arms like a small partner. When I see a book of mine on a shelf in a bookstore, I touch the place where my name is printed.

In poems, paragraphs and chapters, I discover that I know more than I thought I did, that I'm braver and more daring than I believed I could be, that I'm not as different from others as I once believed, and maybe most importantly, that I'm not the idiot girl my father told me I was.

⏤∽⏤

Whatever your life situation—whether you live in a city high-rise or a cabin in the woods, whether you have one parent at home or two or none, whether you know what you want to say or think you've got nothing worth saying—there are poems within you that only you can write. I know that as well as I know the truth of sunlight's warmth against my face on a cold day.

That voice of yours, does it shout? Has it ever hit against a wall, shattering like glass? Or does it whisper, making no more sound than a dream does? Has your voice been yours for a thousand years or are you finding it tonight—your very own voice calling to you—so you can't fall asleep and must write word upon word on the page of night?

What you'll write nobody else will. Nobody else can. You're the only one who knows what you know, who dreams what you dream, the only one who'll turn a phrase just so, who'll follow the word "soul" with "tricks." If you don't write your poems, they will never be written, and the stories of your life will go untold. If you don't write your poems, they'll not even have the substance of smoke. If you don't write your poems, they'll be lost, and with those lost poems go parts of you.

But if you do write your poems, you will find that you have more life, that it will be sturdier than it was before, and truer. The details of the world will catch your attention more than ever. Writing one poem leads to writing another. The weight that pressed against your chest is carried away by a flock of crows. With your words you can stand up for yourself and others, and more than ever the world needs the truths that poems provide.

Chances are this book's in your hands because poetry has called your name. You've got poems under your tongue; they're lurking in the crevices of your days. Don't remain unwritten! Make your indelible stain. Tattoo yourself to the pages of your life.

∞

My Shouting, Shattered, Whispering Voice is divided
into five sections. The first, "Poetry's Calling: Finding
Yourself on Paper," looks at why writers write and
what writing can do for us. We'll explore what gets us
to the page and look at how to deepen our encounters
with writing. The second section, "'If One Part Were
Touched, the Whole Would Tremble': Poetry from the
Inside Out," focuses on poetry's nitty-gritty—line break,
voice and style, punctuation, metaphor and simile. The
book's third section, "Who Said You Couldn't Say That?:
Twenty-Five Poetry-Writing Inspirations in Twenty-
One Short Chapters," will give you lots to write about.
When you're ready to think about giving readings and
publishing your poems, turn to the fourth section,
"'How Possible Might the Impossible Be?': Getting Your
Poetry Out There." The book's last section "Where to Go
from Here: Poetry Resources," consists of a compendium
of websites and a bibliography.

PART I

Poetry's Calling: Finding
Yourself on Paper

*Here's an intimate look at the writing mind
and what writing poetry can do for us.*

1 *Why Write?*

What gets you to the page with a pen between your fingers? What made you crack the spine of this book? If poetry has got you in its grip, lucky you, doomed as you may be to a life of metaphor and small notebooks crammed in the back pocket of *your* jeans. Everyone may have something to say, but not everyone is inclined to write.

You may read plenty, but no one else's words, no matter how close they come to the truth of your experience, will come close enough. Their poem isn't ever going to be yours. Nobody can say what you will in the way you will. And funny thing: the more you write, the more there is to write. Uncovering one layer allows the next layer to emerge. Once you discover that you can take the whirlpool inside and press it onto paper, give it form, and transform your truth into poems, why give that up?

The novelist with the heart of a poet, Zora Neale Hurston, best known for her book *Their Eyes Were Watching God*, put it this way: "I do not know whether you ever went down to the Matanza River in your pigtail days to fish and caught a toad fish. You know if they are swallowed by a big fish, they will eat their way out through the walls of its stomach. That is like the call to write. You must do it irregardless, or it will eat its way out of you anyhow." Kind of a gross way to put it, and yet . . .

Poet Sara Michas-Martin says, "I want to write things down to honor and see things more clearly. To find a choreography for my thoughts. To keep time from sliding away from me. I want to make a simple fruit taste like magic again. Because a Jolly Rancher is delicious, but sometimes you want to experience the actual watermelon. You want to use your teeth to bite down to the rind; you want the cold juice on your chin."

Have you stopped to ask yourself for your very own why? Not that you have to. Being here is enough. Maybe your reasons appear on this list: Write to *write* a wrong; to save yourself; to define; to tell the truth; to refute a lie; to tell a lie; to shout out or speak up, to talk back, to resist; to kiss someone who you can't reach with your actual lips (or who has turned away from your kiss when you stood a mere heartbeat away from each other); to fight with words (a substance more durable and less breakable than fists); to push back your chair (letting it fall behind you) and to stand up, not *as though* for the first time, but *for* the first time, to make your voice sharp and bright as firecrackers in the too-still, too-black night.

Write so you won't disappear, to give up needing to be liked, to stop the burning inside, to honor complication, to contain the uncontainable and make the too-big thing that happened small enough to hold in your hands, to forfeit others' ideas of who you are, to become un-tame, to proclaim, to take flight, to celebrate your rich interior life, to grow your imagination, to stop hurting yourself, to actually love your very own self. Write to disarm silence, to flog fear, to laugh out loud without anyone hearing until you want them to hear, to split as in cells or as in a cord of wood, to puzzle through but not as in crossword or jigsaw.

But past any other why, write to discover and to know.

If you write, you will be able, maybe for the first time, to see what you think and honor how you feel. When in emotional crisis, writing poems can be a beauty-making balm to the soul.

Your words: brilliant birds cutting their way through the slow-to-light dawn. Your words: wind through trees disturbing the disgruntled fog. Your words: truck brakes just in time. Your words: a ladder going up and up and up some more.

And then there's joy.

Let's not go a moment, not a breath further, without it! Joy is often left out of conversations about writing, maybe because for some it's so intrinsic to the experience that it's too obvious to mention, while for others, writing may be a kind of hard labor they're drawn to for the reward of saying what needs to be said. For those writers, joy comes *after* the saying rather than *during*.

To me, the solitary happiness of one word introducing itself to another and how they'll sit together like new best friends on a bus ride, is worth all the parts of writing that challenge, frustrate, and confuse. One word takes a writer to the next one, one phrase leads to the phrase that will follow, and so on.

Writing is a way to bear witness to yourself and the world around you. Writer Isabel Allende put it this way: "I write to preserve memory against the erosion of oblivion. . . . If we listen to another person's story, if we tell our own story, we start to heal from division and hatred, because we realize that the similarities that bring us together are many more than the differences that separate us."

It's like this: a buildup of emotion, a memory, or an occurrence gets a person to the page, all sweaty and out of breath; I mean, finally! For some, it's the moment when you've had enough, too much, really. You pick up the pen, and a change occurs. I write for those moments.

The molten material inside the volcano of you rises up. Now there's fire in the air though nobody else is aware of it. And you take that fire, hot as it is, and singe it to the page, turning it into a poem. If that poem gets lost or you take a match to it, whatever. It's been written, that's the thing. No longer are your words hollow *almosts*.

You've crossed the line between taking and stuffing down what comes at you, and you talk back—in a way that's not likely to cause you trouble. The moment you speak your truth in a poem, you take the first steps to becoming a writer.

You get good at writing by doing three things: reading, writing, and noticing the world around you and the world inside you. Almost anything can be interesting if it's said in a way that grabs attention, tells a truth, says something as it's never been said before. Your way into writing will be your own. To be a writer you don't need to be ordained; you can do it without anyone's blessing (though, just in case, I'm giving you mine).

Writers write because we have something to say, even in those moments when we don't know exactly what it is. What compels you becomes a piece of your "why I write."

The poet Marge Piercy said: "You have to / like it better than being loved." Oh, golly, now that's asking a lot, don't you think? But maybe writing is being loved! It's

4

yourself loving your self with all your crazy facets, and loving life and the world with all its complexities.

Write because you make a promise to write. For me, keeping that promise depends on my listening to all I hear. I was in high school when I made this promise. And it took years for the words to come regularly in an easy, un-tortured kind of way. Wanting to write doesn't mean it's easy.

At first and for a long time in my writing life, the words had to endure hatred—my own, toward myself and toward the words themselves—to get to the page. I told them they weren't the right ones; they were too plain or too flowery or didn't come close enough to what I wanted to say. There was always something mean to say. I wrote half a book with a fight going on between my writer self and the internal critic (whom we'll address later): "I will write you," I persisted. "I can't write you," a voice inside me screamed back.

But those years ago, sitting outside the music building, when I first experienced words coming freely and truly, I loved them. They were much more than flat shapes upon paper. My words were both a mirror and a path to show the way ahead. I promised: *Words, if you come, I'll listen and make a place for you; and with you, I'll make a life.*

The visual artist Louise Nevelson said, "It's a hell of a thing to be born, and if you're born, you're at least entitled to yourself." Being entitled to one's self and to making one's own life—out of words or anything else— wasn't something I saw in the people around me. It wasn't an easy promise to keep. So, what?

I've kept this promise for a good long time, on easy days and troubled ones, and plan to keep it until I am beyond promise keeping, which I hope is many years from now. Through writing I've become a stronger writer, and a more confident one.

Sure, it's a hell of a thing to be born, yet here you are, entitled to yourself. Care to make this writing promise too? If you do, but you want to keep it secret, no worries. I'll believe in your promise even when you don't. And I'll hold your secret close; not a word of it will escape these red lips, ever.

2 Poetry in the Beginning

To orient us a little—and to demonstrate that this poetry thing you and I do has been going on for a very long time, changing as people do—let's take a quick look at poetry's beginning. We are storytelling creatures by nature—through various forms of expression: poetry, fiction, song, painting, sculpture—and this has been so since near the beginning of humanity. We reflect on our experiences, interpret them, and search for meaning through telling the events of our lives.

In her 1993 Nobel Prize for Literature acceptance speech, Toni Morrison said, "Word-work is sublime . . . because it is generative; it makes meaning . . . We die. That may be the meaning of life. But we do language. That may be the measure of our lives." This is true of people throughout every age and from every place in the world—be it Somalia or Kathmandu, the Bronx or Brooklyn. It's true of those who write books and those who tell bedtime stories.

Morrison said, "Narrative is radical, creating us at the very moment it is being created." In other words, we *are* the stories we tell. By taking control of the telling, those of us who write get, at least in part, to determine the stories that are told about us.

Long before events such as lightning and earthquakes were scientifically understood, poems, songs, and stories were created and shared as a way to make sense of what had no comprehensible explanation. If you sing a song about, say, lightning and what it might mean, it becomes less overwhelming. Maybe you say there's a god of lightning. Maybe you say that god makes strikes in the sky because she's angry. Again, from Morrison's speech: "Language alone protects us from the scariness of things with no name."

Poems have marked our way for eons, serving to chronicle events, to explain the inexplicable, to educate and enlighten, to warn others of danger, to celebrate life and love, to proclaim triumphs, to declare love and lament heartbreak, to cope with defeat, and to mourn loss and tragedy.

Before human beings developed writing, before poems were written down on either stone or papyrus, poetry was a spoken art form, taking the form of prayer, chants, hymns, and songs. In Africa, poetry was used to help hunters as far back as prehistoric times. If a group of hunters encountered a big, scary animal, chanting a poem together could fortify their strength and help them cope with their fear. In Africa, as well, poems were, and are, a performance art included in tribal ceremonies.

Early people had deep a conviction in the magic properties of words and believed that particular phrases spoken aloud could affect outcomes. Today, the belief that words can have tremendous power rightly persists. In his poem "Magic Words," the Inuit poet Nalungiaq said: "A word spoken by chance / might have strange consequences. / It would suddenly come alive."

By using language to go beyond language, poetry creates something larger and more mysterious than a simple collection of words. Ursula K. Le Guin affirmed this by saying, "All makers must leave room for the acts of the spirit."

The early poems weren't considered to have individual authors but were a shared part of the culture. Passed down from one generation to the next, their content changed over time. Repetition and rhythm helped people to remember them. Once the skill of writing had been developed, poems began to belong to individual writers, because one person could sit alone and craft language on their own.

Two of the world's first identified poets were women. The ancient Akkadian poet Enheduanna, a high priestess who lived in the twenty-third century BCE, is the first writer known to sign her name to her work. The Greek poet Sappho wrote poems and songs during the sixth century BCE.

Overall, contemporary poems focus less than the early poems did on religious and community concerns; they tend to be more interested in the individual and the individual in community, and it is through these personal narratives that they speak to others.

What every one of us who takes up the pen to answer poetry's call has in common—from the ancient times to the present—is a desire to respond, to assert our truths, to talk back to the darkness, and to celebrate the light.

9

3   *The Mind of the Poet*

Since I was a little girl, I've felt pulled to notice the moments when what's hinted at goes unsaid. You know how it is when you feel a vague tension between people in a room or you barely see a flicker-y movement out of the corner of your eye? I was convinced that life was full of almost-hidden secrets and mystery. Children dwell in curiosity, wonder, and possibility.

When we are very young and still getting to know the world, our knowledge of what's real and what's not isn't fixed. Kids think magically as a way to make sense of what they don't yet understand. Children tend to be more openhearted and open-minded, and less rigid, than adults. The realm of spirit, which tends to reduce as we grow up, is something that many children have easy access to.

Poets and artists are people who maintain a relationship with mystery for their entire lives. They don't discredit what can't be explained. They pay attention to subtle connections and interactions between people (how someone raised his eyebrow for an instant and what it might have meant) and in their environment (the way one tree leans into another).

Not only do we acknowledge that not all of life is within the realm of rational understanding, but we celebrate it. We never stop wishing on stars. We are taken by life's supposedly insignificant miracles, little pieces of daily magic. The poet has a bit of the sorcerer, the inventor, and the shaman within.

The other day I was listening to a podcast while driving. The man speaking was talking about the people he looked up to, whom he referred to as his giants. That got me thinking of my own such people. When I stopped at a red light, I saw that the license plate on the car ahead of me spelled out G I A N T. Just an unexplainable synchronicity, a bit of magic, and I loved it.

The poet Emily Dickinson said, "Tell all the truth but tell it slant—," meaning, be truthful but original. The poet's mind tends toward the slant. The writer recognizes the extraordinary within the ordinary and believes life is full of secrets that can only be uncovered, if they are to be uncovered, by writing them. They may fall in love a thousand times a day; when in love, time is not made up of hours but of glances.

The writer never sleeps. I don't mean that literally, of course. I mean that, even asleep, the writer is engaged in writing because, come morning, a dream that upended her becomes the basis for a new poem. Within everything that occurs—what we think and feel, and all that we witness—there might be a poem.

Poets (and other sensitive people) have a kind of radar, like the antennae that crickets and bees have, to feel out what's ahead and around us, so we can notice the smallest of shifts. Writers tend to have a lot of empathy—they feel what others are going through. This leads me to think that the lives of those of us who write are more deeply inhabited and more fully examined.

The writer not only notices what transpires but responds to it, because it's something that's caused her to feel or think deeply. Maybe a stranger looked at her and turned her heart into a butterfly. Or say she's denied access to a place where others freely go because of her age, gender, ethnicity, race, or nationality. So she stands under a street-light, feverishly loading the details onto her phone.

The writer reflects, questions, writes past the over-story—what's most obvious—and far into the under-story, attentive to nuance and complication. In this way, the writer finds out how she feels about it.

To write, one needs a willingness to be without an answer for hours or days, and to remain curious, to be drawn to what is unexplainable, to be mesmerized by ephemeral connections. One phrase propels you into the arms of another.

Nikola Tesla, best known for designing modern alternating current electricity systems (and for having a car named after him!), said: "If you want to find the secrets of the universe, think in terms of energy, frequency, and vibration." To be a poet, give your *energy* to writing, write *frequently*, and you will become skilled at tuning in to subtle *vibrations* that hold the secrets to life.

Ultimately, it's the poet who, no matter how old he gets, never loses a sense of the child's amazement about life. In her poem "When Death Comes," Mary Oliver said it well:

> *When it's over, I want to say: all my life*
> *I was a bride married to amazement.*

If you don't need the grandiose in order to feel
amazed, but are moved by occurrences as small as a
falling leaf or the asking expression in your dog's eyes,
with your attentive poet's mind you will find material for
poems, because poetry is everywhere and all the time.

4 What Writing Does for Us

If I hadn't found poetry, many experiences, though
well lived, would have gone from my memory.
Certain events have nuggets of gold in them to carry
us through the lean times. When troubling things
happen, writing can help us to come to grips with
what's confusing and can free us from holding on
to the difficult. If we write a poem about something
pleasurable, we make it linger.

The first time my husband and I kissed, we stood waist
deep in cold water—I'd led him into a redwood forest to
a hidden cold spring. After slipping into the icy water, I
looked up at him expectantly, waiting for him to join me.
Our kiss turned into a poem, "First Kiss," that ends:

> *You tasted of wood smoke and honey.*
> *You tasted of my future,*
> *and I liked that.*

Even my feet did.
They would have to walk
no further.

Some years before that, I spent the last days of my
mother's life beside her in a hospital's intensive care unit.
The pocket of my jacket held a notebook and a pencil.

The moment I'd first walked into her hospital room,
she'd been, with great effort, waking from a coma, and
said, "You haven't been to dinner lately, how come?"—
never remembering that she had cast me out of her life
five years before, after I'd told her I was in love with a
woman.

During the next several days, before she slipped back
into the coma, I attempted to make up for our lost time.
While sitting beside her, singing her favorite songs,
recalling the mother who once had a twinkle in her eye
and danced a mean Irish jig, I was also writing.

When I want to get that time back, I open my first
book of poems and there are those nine days, in black on
white. As difficult as that time was, I don't want to lose it.
Those were the last days my mother and I had together.

"At first, as a teenager," poet Safia Elhillo told me,
poetry "was a form of journaling, with the verse/lyric
of it acting as a sort of smoke screen or alibi if my mom
ever read my notebook! It helped me make sense of my
thoughts and my feelings by holding me accountable to
naming them. It helped me feel more rooted in my expe-
riences, in the world as it happened to me, by making
me work to think of the specific word for each sensation,
each emotion, each action."

The writer's job is to pay attention to himself and to the details of the world. Writing hones the skill of observation. The other day, I parked my car to run errands and noticed a well-dressed elderly man standing on the sidewalk next to a small tree that was losing its leaves to autumn. He picked up a fallen leaf from the sidewalk, found a nook in the tree, and placed it there. "That's better," he said to me, smiling, before he walked on.

The more we notice the details of each other, the more we may come to realize that the separating line is dotted instead of solid. The elderly man and his leaf have been with me for days now. I love the way the page holds them and gives them back to me.

Safia Elhillo went on to say, "Writing poetry is one of my favorite forms of play. I love to stretch and examine the possibilities of language, the edges of language, the failings of language. I love to challenge my own ideas about what I can and cannot do in a poem, to challenge everything I learned about what I am and am not allowed to do in a poem. Growing up bilingual made language my great fascination as well as my great trauma, and writing poetry has been a way to find a sense of curiosity, of play, in my sort of traumatizing lifelong pursuit of fluency."

5   Belief in the Unwritten

Everybody has an imagination—it's a vital part of our sophisticated minds. For some, the imagination is active, and for others, not so much. The more you use your imagination, the stronger it will get, like a muscle.

As much as it's an essential part of being a writer, the imagination is pretty darn important for nearly everyone. We engage it when we search for a solution to a problem we're stuck on. Say you're hungry but there are only two ingredients left in the cupboard: peanut butter and a garlic clove, and the fridge holds only a bunch of carrots and a few slices of bread, your imagination will help you figure out what to make for dinner, or at least for a snack. Scientists rely on theirs too. Debaters need theirs to win a debate. Doctors to find remedies to heal the sick. Kids to explain misdeeds. And on and on it goes.

15

Because imagining is an invisible act, and because in some circles it's not viewed as being as essential as rational, intellectual, and analytical thought, even the most imaginative among us may struggle to put our faith in it, especially before there's anything on paper. Our imaginations can be undermined by our own negativity, or by another's.

When you were little, did anyone ever say to you, "Stop, you're just imagining that!"? As though pretending wasn't a good thing! The most logical among us love to question and disbelieve what isn't easily verifiable.

To grow your imagination, celebrate and engage it. When you write a poem, you give your imagination form. Part of creating the conditions for your writing to prosper means putting faith in the thing that doesn't yet exist—the unwritten poem.

American poet W. S. Merwin said it this way at the beginning of his poem "The Unwritten":

> *Inside this pencil*
> *crouch words that have never been written*
> *never been spoken*
> *never been thought*
>
> *they're hiding . . .*

Because a poem is as of yet unwritten doesn't mean it's not real—doesn't mean it's not on its way. Maybe look at it as my former ninth-grade student Monica E. did in these lines:

> *This poem knows you.*
> *It is reading you*
> *between its lines . . .*

I think Monica was right. Our yet-to-be-written poems may know us better than we know ourselves.

6   *The Blue Mountains Far Away:*
The Art of Listening

There's the listening we do when we're hungry and waiting to be called in for dinner, which is different from the listening done by the one who's calling to you from the kitchen window while stirring supper on the stove. Neither of those is like wishing to be called in for dinner and listening for the call that won't come.

How often we listen not for the words themselves but

for what's beneath or beyond them, the thing your friend wants to say but can't. I had a close friend in high school who suffered at the hands of her older brother, but she didn't tell me or our other close friend until many years later—too late for us to be of help when she needed it most. I think she was trying to tell us back then, but in ways I didn't know how to listen for.

The kind of listening a poet does is one of the deepest kinds there is. Poems may require us to listen beyond ourselves in order to make our work whole and true, to incorporate the delight and strife present in our surroundings and communities.

Ever try to tune in to a station on an old-fashioned radio, maybe a car radio, moving the knob ever so slowly? Especially when driving through rural places, there's a sound that comes over the radio like paper crackling loudly on either side of the music you so badly want to hear. You have to adjust the dial precisely to get the music to come in clearly. I think of writing-listening like that.

Here's how it goes for me when I sit down to write. I lean a little to the side, always the right side. My sweetheart isn't arriving on the noon train, so I'm not listening for him but to a voice that comes from the blue mountains far away. Somewhere out in the distance, words are being whispered that only I can hear. Poems can be shy as untamed animals. They approach in their own time and don't like to be rushed. You may have to listen closely to hear what's calling you.

A friend of mine likens writing to lifting up rocks in the hills out behind her house. That wouldn't work for me, because I'd be afraid that under those rocks a bunch of snakes might begin to writhe and slither. But she's fearless: she lifts up the rocks, has never been bitten once, and finds her poems there, whole and true.

Often as I'm writing one phrase, I'll hear the next one coming, ready for the paper. This may sound crazy, or you may already know what I mean—or have your own version of the experience. The more you write, the clearer your process will become. Trusting in it and tuning in helps a lot.

Much of my last nonfiction book, *Step into Nature*, was written while out walking in the five-hundred-acre wood not far from home. I began going there in order to write, having discovered that the words could find me more easily at a distance from email and internet searches. For me, nature offers a purer space than any within four walls. At first, I wrote notes on my hand. It wasn't, slow learner that I am, until the day the ink went halfway up my arm that I considered carrying a small notebook with me.

Some of us need quiet to be able to hear the words that are coming, but a lot of writers do their best work in a bustling café. Once you practice this kind of listening often enough, you may find that you're out with friends or in class—otherwise occupied—when you hear the poetry voice speaking a line in your head. It's come when my hands have been in hot soapy water or when driving a car. Mostly when I'm alone but not always.

Hearing the truth can be difficult—more complicated than is desired, more intimate than is comfortable. Poetry, with its symbolism and imagery, its ability to hold complexity in a few words, is an ideal form for telling whatever truths you're drawn to listen for. The more you listen, the more there is to hear.

7 *Kinds of Silence*

You know the silence that comes over you when listening to new music or looking into the eyes of somebody whom, maybe, you love? There's the silence of listening to the churning ocean during a storm. And the way lightning makes us silent as we wait for the thunder. My least favorite is the weighted silence that comes from another after I've said more than I should have.

For writers, there are times when silence matters more than words. Into that silence you put your listening for what comes next, or you put your not listening because you're recovering from and assimilating what you've recently written. Writers talk about fallow periods. Like flowers in a garden, we can't bloom all the time. We need to rest, to fill the well of creativity.

At such times, if someone asks me, "Are you writing?" beads of sweat start to form and my face gets red. I'm thinking, "No, damn it, I'm not writing a thing," and I'll get all guilty feeling inside as though I were in the wrong—in the wrong about *my* writing. Maybe there's something on the tip of my tongue that I keep biting in order to avoid it. Or maybe it's one of those necessary quiet times.

The American poet Audre Lorde said, "Your silence

will not protect you." The kind of silence she's talking about is not one of those fallow times. She's referring to how we can use silence to avoid telling a necessary truth—either on the page to ourselves, or in our lives. If those untold stories, those unwritten poems need to be told, their weight will press upon us. Getting to know your silences, to distinguish between their various kinds, is almost as much a part of writing as putting your fingers on the keyboard.

8   Truth, Lies and Poetry

A poem is one way to assert your truth, and writing a poem will lead you to the depths of your truths as only a poem can.

If you are growing up in a family where not everyone is honest, or if elsewhere in your life you're lied to and told that it's the truth, it's terribly confusing, especially for children. If there is alcohol or drug abuse, what is real and true may feel slippery and not easily verifiable.

In the family I come from, my mother's addiction to alcohol and her mental instability caused her sense of reality to frequently shift. It was as though at one moment the couch was blue and the next it was red. She wasn't deliberately lying to me; her reality was in flux.

Children are sophisticated observers. To get by, I became alert to the alterations in my mother's behavior and speech, in order to judge her state of mind. When her tongue was thick in her mouth and she was overly and uncharacteristically affectionate or on the verge of unwarranted anger, when her step was clumsy, I learned to keep my distance, to ask nothing from her.

When life is unpredictable due to adults being unreliable or for any reason, young people can have a difficult time trusting their own perceptions. If you are pretty sure about something but the person in charge tells you, "Nope, that's wrong," it's difficult not to question yourself.

My early experiences caused me to turn inward. I began to hone an imagination. It was safe there because it was my own place; I could trust it. Whatever I can say about the difficulties of my early life, it was great preparation for becoming a writer.

We are currently living at a time when truth and facts are being questioned and denied in a large arena: that of our country. When someone in power says that they don't "believe" that global warming is caused by human activity, despite what the facts of science have proven, that's crazy-making. It's one thing to believe or not believe in something unverifiable or subjective, and it's another thing to believe or not believe in facts. Facts do not require belief. They simply are.

Here's how Jane Hirshfeld opens her poem "On the Fifth Day":

> *On the fifth day*
> *the scientists who studied rivers*
> *were forbidden to speak*
> *or to study rivers.*

She's not writing a speculative fiction–based poem but responding to a governmental mandate, because the facts were not in line with the propaganda being put forth as fact. Further into Hirshfield's poem comes this:

22

> *Someone, from deep in the Badlands,*
> *began posting facts.*
>
> *The facts were told not to speak*
> *and were taken away.*
> *The facts, surprised to be taken, were silent.*

Hirshfield is speaking a necessary truth, and she's being listened to—her poem appeared in the *Washington Post*.

It is true that there is often not a single story but many. The facts *can* depend on the perspective of who's relaying them. If you see a car accident from outside the car, your viewpoint will be different from that of the people inside the car; and, even from inside, the driver may have one view and the people in the backseat another. But everyone should be able to recognize that, yes, unfortunately, there was a car accident.

When it comes to writing poetry, ah, the beautiful complications! If you're writing about something that actually happened, the facts may be important but the main thing is to use language to convey your *sense* of the experience, to focus your poem on that. Maya Angelou put it this way: "There's a world of difference between truth and facts. Facts can obscure the truth." The poem is going for the heart of the moment, its essence as expressed through you.

In a poem by Lawrence Ferlinghetti called "Fortune Has Its Cookies to Give Out" he recalls a childhood memory of a hot summer day in Brooklyn when the firemen closed the street and turned on their hoses:

> *and all the kids ran out in it*
> *in the middle of the street*
> *and there were*
>
>   *maybe a couple dozen of us*
>   *out there*
> *with the water squirting up*
>   *to the*
>   *sky*
> *and all over*
>   *us . . .*

As the poem continues, Ferlinghetti begins adjusting the number of kids who were there from twelve to six.

Ferlinghetti, a poet who turned one hundred years old in 2019, didn't set out to fib when he wrote that there were a dozen kids on the street. That's how, as he thought back to the experience, he remembered it. The event was significant and that's how it felt. About midway through the poem, as more of the memory returns to him, he writes that the kids outside "were in our barefeet and birthday suits," bringing more of the memory back to him. The poems ends:

> *While I remember Molly*
> > *looked at me and*
> *ran in*
> *because I guess really we were the only ones there.*

Memory tends to come back at a sensory level first; it's the *feel* of what happened that we initially recall. Ponder a memory, and you'll bring it into greater focus. By writing his poem this way, Ferlinghetti makes us privy to his experience of the process of remembering.

One of my favorite lines of poetry comes from E. E. Cummings: "nobody,not even the rain,has such small hands." Can you feel the line's resonance even though it's entirely impossible and illogical? Poems embrace a truth larger than what's obvious, one that seeks to welcome the most authentic awareness possible.

When writing a poem, facts enter in through the unlocked front door (as they should be able to). Truth comes in through the cracks in the door or a broken window. A poem is after truth, and since you're its author, *your* truth in particular. The poem and your life experiences belong to you. This isn't going to be your father's poem nor the one your best friend would write. It's yours, and isn't that nice?

By speaking your truth, you make way for others to do the same. Adrienne Rich said, "When a woman tells the truth she is creating the possibility for more truth around her." This is so whatever your gender. If you're a member of a group whose truth hasn't been accepted as accurate or valid by the mainstream, then speaking your truth has greater importance and may make truth telling possible for others.

9   *How Do You Know?*

When writing a poem, all your ways of knowing and understanding yourself and the world come into play. Let's look at some of the ways in which we come to know what we know.

   * There's what you know because it's been told to you and, since you trust the teller, you accept what they've said—so much so that it becomes your knowledge too.

   * You have plenty of firsthand knowledge—all that you have experienced yourself.

   * Dreams impart their knowing, even before we realize or understand their meaning. I don't yet know the meaning of the dream of four wolves that I had last night, but I trust that an understanding is working through me and will come as near as the wolves themselves did.

   * There's school learning, with the accompanying reading, research, and studying, as well as what you learn about people there.

   * Your body knows things and will tell you, if you listen. From our bodies we can obtain a multitude of information. Your feet know the ground is soft, and your hands know that guy's face is. Hunger brings its knowledge. Breath offers another. Cut skin teaches us pain.

Even emotional pain may be felt in the body, the way the heart gets heavy when we're sad.

* Your imagination has its own knowing. It can deepen your other ways of knowing, inspiring pictures, poems, stories.

26

* Recent research shows that not only do physical traits and skills get passed down, but emotional ones do too, like a tendency toward melancholy. After my mother's death, I inherited my grandmother's Boston rocker and noticed how the black paint on the chair's arms was worn off where the hands rest. For months, I sat rocking back and forth thinking of my mother, feeling sad. That made me wonder about how easily I can slip into sorrow, and how my mother could. My grandmother's life had more than a little sorrow too. Did she sit in that rocker when she was sad?

Do you come from a people who have had to flee repeatedly over time? The knowledge of that tenuousness may well be a part of who you are.

When writing, you can welcome your many ways of knowing. If you get stuck in the process, ask your hands what they know about the memory you're giving voice to. What would your ancestors say? Engage your five senses.

10   The Five Senses

Our five senses are our first introductions to the world, as soon as—and even before—we're born. While in utero, the fetus comes to recognize the voices most often heard and, once born, babies will know not only their mother's voice but her scent as being uniquely hers. Much of what we encounter comes to us through our five senses. We learn early that the jarring sound of glass breaking usually means something's wrong. The taste of butter, with or without the popcorn, is for many people the ultimate in delicious comfort, while some take to honey and still others are sated most by a salty something on the tongue.

Take a look at these excerpts from Theodore Roethke's "My Papa's Waltz":

> *The whiskey on your breath*
> *Could make a small boy dizzy;*
> . . . .
> *We romped until the pans*
> *Slid from the kitchen shelf;*
> . . . .
> *You beat time on my head*
> *With a palm caked hard by dirt,*
> *Then waltzed me off to bed*
> *Still clinging to your shirt.*

So sensory a poem! Can you smell that whiskey—sour and not tasty? Can you hear the pots clanging to the floor, see the hand, and feel the thumping on your head?

Though I've read the poem many times, reading it again dizzies me.

Many years ago, when my mother and her sisters were little girls, back when there was no electric refrigeration, the iceman would make deliveries in his horse-drawn cart. On hot days, the girls would run after the cart, picking up the ice chips that fell off it and sucking on them till they melted. One such day, my aunt picked up what turned out not to be ice, but a piece of glass, and she swallowed the small jagged bit whole. Notice how that story comes in at the throat! The family was worried, but my aunt was unharmed.

Introduce sensory words into your writing and you'll increase the immediacy, the intimacy, and the intensity of the experience you're describing. When you want to write about the way you feel emotionally, and if you're struggling to convey it, ask yourself, "If I could taste this feeling, what would it taste like?"

11 The Sixth Sense: Intuitive Knowing

A friend of mine was in bed for weeks, far too young to be dying, but there she was. I'd sit with her and we'd watch Charlie Chaplin movies and chat. One afternoon, upon waking from a nap, Rosmarie said, "Patrice, Susan's at the door. Please answer it." Nobody had knocked so I looked at my friend quizzically. "Go on," she said, waving me away. Before I got to the door, there was a knock. Upon my opening it, Susan walked in.

A little while later, with panic in her voice, Rosmarie said, "Patrice, my brother is calling from Switzerland." "But the phone isn't ringing." "Patrice, get me the telephone!" (She was never the most patient of people, but in dying she was at her impatient best.) I reached for the phone as it began to ring, handing it to my friend. "Ollie, how good to hear from you," she said.

29

There's a word to describe having foreknowledge: prescience. Chilean poet Gabriela Mistral, who won the Nobel Prize for Literature in 1945 (the first Latin American to win and only the fifth woman to receive one), explained it this way:

> *Spelling out the unseen,*
> *giving names to the foretold . . .*

Perhaps you've had a dream while asleep, and the next day what you dreamed of occurs. Or maybe you've had a sense when awake that something was going to happen and then it did. Then there's the experience of déjà vu—you're doing something and you have the distinct sense that the exact same thing has happened before. What's odder still is when this happens with two people at the same time.

For the most part, we experience time as being sequential, though physicists tell us otherwise. Einstein said, "The distinction between past, present, and future is only a stubbornly persistent illusion." Intuition brings time's linearity into question.

In part, intuition consists of deep, concentrated attention. If you're open and alert not only to what you expect to happen but also to the dazzlement you can't imagine, you may find yourself more aware than you knew you could be. When writing, employ all your ways of knowing to describe experience. Poetry brings out what's hidden and that which has gone unnoticed, disregarded, or deprived of respect. Peer behind the curtain and you might find that, unlike in *The Wizard of Oz*, there's magic taking place.

30

12   *Inviting Inspiration*

Say you're writing and ideas for what to write keep coming one after another as though you're taking dictation; it's like you're communing with an invisible sensibility. You're saying things you couldn't have imagined you would, attentive to words because you *want* to be, not because a teacher or parent is telling you to be. Other things may be going on in the room around you, but they're barely noticeable: that's because you're inspired and in the flow.

Inspiration comes as the result of noticing your surroundings, of listening, of trusting your intuition and your own inclinations about what to write, plus an extra inexplicable something. There are many things about life to be in awe of. Inspiration is one of them. When I feel inspired, it's like being in love, a swoony kind of light-headed, hard-to-catch-my-breath feeling.

I like how Safia Elhillo defines inspiration as a natural part of the writing and thinking process by saying,

"I now just think of my brain finishing its incubation process for an idea that has been nesting in me for a while—finishing that partially subconscious process and pushing it into the realm of work, of something I have to sit down and work out."

"Inspire" comes from the Latin *inspirare*, meaning "to inhale." A writer inhales life and exhales poetry. Toni Morrison said, "Everything I see or do, the weather and the water, buildings . . . everything *actual* is an advantage when I am writing. It is like a menu, or a giant tool box, and I can pick and choose what I want." Inspiration allows us to see the ordinary anew.

31

Though inspiration is not something you can go looking for—the mindset of searching is pretty much its antithesis—you can set up welcoming conditions. Experiencing inspiration has a lot to do with receptivity and anticipation. In Antoine de Saint-Exupéry's book *The Little Prince*, when the little prince arrives to visit the fox for a second time, the fox says, "It would have been better to have come back at the same hour. . . . If, for example, you come at four o'clock in the afternoon, then at three o'clock, I shall begin to be happy. I shall feel happier as the hour advances."

Predawn mornings are my favorite time to write: not only is the day fresh and new—at my house, nobody's awake except the cats, who pad beside me to my room and curl up nearby while I'm writing—but my mind is clearest then and my heart less battered by the day, and I don't yet need to address the business of living. Some love late nights—the quiet it offers; that's the time of day when they feel free. If you experiment with writing at different times of day, you'll discover what works for you.

Consider making a schedule, not a daunting one, but one you find reasonable. Say you decide to write every Saturday afternoon from 2:00 to 2:30? Start with what easily fits your life and doesn't overwhelm you. Thirty minutes may turn into an hour. Every Saturday, there you are with your tablet or your pencil, ready to write.

If a little idea wiggles up like a worm in the dirt, take it. If you say, "Oh, you're only a slimy little worm; I want something bigger, better," inspiration may grab that idea and slither back underground with it, leaving you with white emptiness.

But if you approach what appears to be a bit of insignificance with an attitude of curiosity—"Okay, let's see here"—and you begin writing, soon other words, phrases, and sentences will join. Later, once an entire page is filled with material you didn't know you had in you, you may thank that initial little worm. Even when I'm hesitant, tired, doubtful, busy with other things (whatever the roadblock is to sitting down and writing), if I begin, one word is lonely on the page and invites her friends and, because they love her, they come. A whole village of words may join you before that half hour is up.

My experience tells me that, like the people in our lives, inspiration, as an aspect of the creative process, wants to be trusted, to be waited for and admired, wants us to show up when we say we will. Truly, this is about being present to the deepest part of yourself so you can respond to what's there. A schedule may support you greatly.

If you create a routine that suits you, but, after a while, you begin to resent it, it's time to let go of that predictability, at least for now. Maybe at this point, spontaneity is the thing to support your writing. Once I heard a poet say that she waits for inspiration to come, and then she sits down. I admire that she's able to stop what she's in the middle of and turn to the approaching poem. She must be particularly sensitive to her inner poet.

Inspiration has caused me to pull over when driving to take its dictation. But if I'm engaged in a kiss, say, I'm as unavailable to inspiration as I should be. Or if I'm enjoying a delicious meal. Or when in the middle of teaching a class of budding poets. Anything that we give our all to may keep inspiration at bay. But times of deep engagement can also lead to inspiration, because those are often the experiences you'll want to write about.

Make way for inspiration, not only by scheduling writing time but also by reading poems that others have written. They remind us of a less pragmatic way of thinking, one that's fluid. When I read poetry, I'm reminded of the value of what I'm engaged in, so that even when words don't come easily, reading a poem or two demonstrates that others have stuck with their writing, and probably lost and regained inspiration too. A particular word combination or another poet's writing inspires my own.

If you come to a point when, poof, inspiration and all ideas for writing have walked out on you, and you feel lost in your writing, don't despair! This is a writer's conundrum. It may be that you've come to a roadblock because you hit against something difficult to say or that you don't yet have language for. If it's not the right time to write it, that's fine. Maybe you've taken that poem as far as it can go for the time being.

Some of us have an inner drill sergeant who says, "Keep going! Don't stop!" And that approach may work. But if it doesn't, if you continually feel like you're only treading water and are almost drowning, give yourself a break.

Einstein described the experience of puzzling and puzzling over a scientific problem. Not coming up with anything, he'd go for a walk, and after a while, as though he'd walked right up to it, there was the answer he'd spent hours or days searching for. When Einstein stopped pushing for his answer, when he relaxed and let his mind go free, what he was searching for came to him.

Stare out the window with a soft focus. Take a solitary walk or a nap if you're tired. "I dream my painting and I paint my dream" may or may not have been said by the artist Vincent Van Gogh. In any case, it's good advice. A nap will take you out of your daily, task-driven mind and into a softer mind. Food's a good idea, if you're hungry. Pet your dog. Inspiration will return to you; I know that it will.

13   Who and What Defines You?

When we're children, we're defined, in great part, by the adults in our lives. They observe us growing into ourselves: "Oh, Berta, she's so outgoing," or "Gabriel's very shy," etc. Sometimes the adults in young people's lives define them in the ways they wish to be defined themselves.

My father was a frustrated artist—he wanted to sculpt and paint, but something inside him was like a wedge between his desire and his ability to pick up a paintbrush. As his young daughter, of course, I didn't know this about him. Art was my favorite thing to do, and what I knew intuitively is that my dad both loved and hated this about me. There I was, a little kid having fun with a box of crayons, free of pressure about how my picture "should" look.

35

When I was in the first grade, there was a school-wide art competition. He'd read the paper I'd brought home and, taking for granted that I'd want to participate, said, "What would you like to draw?" I wasn't particularly interested in drawing *anything*.

He got out a big piece of paper and my big box of crayons. I said I'd draw a ballerina. My father sat at my elbow, coaxing me, and getting frustrated by my inability, at age six, to draw straight lines freehand. He raised his voice, took the pencil from my hand, and began to draw the lines himself.

Eventually the picture did get finished. I did some. He did some. I felt confused by it, turned it in, and won second prize in the show. That prize embarrassed me because it wasn't actually mine.

The following year, when the competition was announced and my father asked me what I'd draw, I was old enough and determined enough to tell him, "I'll do it myself." When he sat down beside me I refused to pick up a crayon. "What do you want to draw?" he asked. "Nothing," I said. One afternoon when he was at work, I drew something; a child feels obliged to please her father, even when she doesn't wholly want to. Because my heart wasn't it, I drew uninspired rolling green hills against a blank, unpainted sky. Of course, no prize was mine, as I knew it wouldn't be, and I was most relieved.

I might have become a visual artist. But because the experience of making pictures had gotten sullied and convoluted, I needed a form that hadn't been "taken" by someone in my family. My mother raised me on poetry— reading and reciting it. But, thank goodness, she didn't write it or expect me to do so. When high school came along, poetry was ready and waiting for me.

At a certain point, as we enter our teen years, many of us want to rebuff definitions imposed on us by even the most well-meaning adults. We're starting to reflect more and more on who we are, who we're becoming, and who we *want* to be.

The point of my story is to encourage you to define yourself; you're the one who gets that right, no matter how your family or your friends or anyone else may see you. While you're living in your parents' home, you may not get to be your whole self, but later you will. If anyone has told you you're not a poet but in your heart of hearts you feel inclined toward poetry, that's what matters. May you define yourself in alliance with your deepest self. Ultimately, it doesn't matter if others—even those you love and respect—don't define you as a poet. What matters is how you define yourself, and that definition is based on who you authentically are and what you do.

Author Roxane Gay says, "Through writing, I was, finally, able to get respect for the content of my character." Respect from others may come to you also, but what's most important is that, like Gay, you give voice to the content of your character. You'll experience self-respect by defining yourself.

14   Responding to a Complicated World

Writing about something that's unsettled you is a great way to come to grips with it and to understand it better. Whether it's positive (a kiss that you didn't anticipate) or negative (witnessing a friend's mistreatment), writing about it can give you a way to process the experience. How often I've written material that's surprised me because I wasn't aware that I thought or felt that way until the pen got going.

Though at times life can be enough to break your heart, you can un-break it (or at least mend it) by writing what you know is true, and, in that way, not only understand it more fully but also take a stand, draw your line—not in sand, but in that which won't be erased when the tide comes in.

Depending on our subjects and how we write about them, writing a poem can, in and of itself, be a political act. Years ago, when I was nineteen, I made a difficult decision. It was a private thing, and for a long time, I didn't consider writing about it because I wasn't sure how to do so. One day, when I was alone in the house with plenty of free time, the poem showed itself to me. As I wrote, the honesty of my telling made me cry, letting me know that I'd hit a nerve that had been previously hidden.

The poem was the story of my abortion. Choosing to terminate my pregnancy was the right decision. I'd been a young, single woman with a drug problem. Not only was I in no position, financially or otherwise, to raise a child alone, I didn't want to have a child—not then, or later.

I am unhesitating in my belief that women have the right to make choices for themselves and their bodies, whether it's to keep or terminate a pregnancy or any other decision. By writing a poem about choosing abortion, I told a significant story, and by publishing "Pregnant," first in a literary journal and then in my second collection of poetry, I publicly took an important stand.

"Little swimmer," I said,
"find yourself
another ocean."

What was I to do with you?
My future was the breathing in of snow.
My history a book I slapped shut
each night.

And though I practiced your name
behind closed doors,
I refused you.

What are the moments in your life, those small or large turning points, that made an emotional, and possibly a political, shift take place? No matter how difficult the telling, if a story presses against you, asking for your words, your truth telling, perhaps you will be ready to stand up with strength, honesty, vigor, and compassion— for yourself and others.

15   *Your Own Company: Writing and Solitude*

The company you're becoming more and more intimate with through writing poems is your own. When you're solo, experiences come to you firsthand. Take walks alone if you live where it's safe to do so. Go out for a coffee by yourself and write about who you see around you. Get up earlier than everyone else in your house or stay up later in order to have time to absorb, reflect, and respond. If you're uncomfortable being alone, with pencil and paper in hand, try it out in small doses.

Take poetry breaks from your devices, five minutes at first and then as many minutes as you can. I'll bet you'll have times when you're so caught up in writing that your phone gets (temporarily) forgotten.

You could also team up with friends who write. Sitting beside each other, you can be alone together. There's a seductive synergy that happens when writing in the company of others; a magical transmission of creativity and inspiration can occur. Two people with their heads bent to their laptops and their fingers clicking away validates the importance of this activity. If you doubt yourself, look up at your friend who is so engrossed he doesn't notice your glance, or who gives you a fleeting, knowing smile. Then you're both back at it.

There's a big difference between being alone and feeling lonely. When I'm writing, I'm never lonely because I'm not entirely by myself; I'm also with the material I'm writing. *Choosing* to be by yourself is an empowering choice, and not at all like being *unchosen* by another.

The first time I felt a kind of holiness in being alone, I was in a cabin during a deep-snow winter in a tiny Northern California town surrounded by forest. Warm inside on that snowy day—I'd just thrown a log into the wood stove—I was comfortably enclosed in the silent house.

As I listened to the fire spitting with a notebook open on my lap, a poem rushed toward me whole. The ears of my ears were listening, the eyes of my eyes were suddenly able to see more truly than before. If friends had been around, likely the patterns of the light would have gone unnoticed; we'd have been too attentive to each other's company.

I was seventeen years old, having recently moved out of my mother's home, a time rife with anxiety and random fear, when being alone was typically anything but comfortable. But on that morning, I felt more alive than I'd ever been.

If you don't like being alone, here are a few suggestions:

* Put your hands or bare feet on a bit of earth for a moment and name all the things you see: sky, tree, scampering cat.

* Bring that air as far into your lungs as you can, and when you exhale, do so slowly, imagining the sense of being overwhelmed going out with your breath.

* Take a quick run or a walk.

* Tell yourself you'll stay focused on writing for only five or ten minutes more, and keep that promise.

41

When writing, solitude is good but isolation isn't, so don't stay away too long and check in with friends when you need support.

16 The "Evils" of Procrastination

For as much as I've practiced procrastination, I could have gotten a second bachelor's degree in it. Do you also tend to avoid and postpone doing things that you find difficult? Do you want to write poems but find the challenge daunting?

Mayo Oshin wrote about the method the French novelist Victor Hugo used to overcome procrastination. In 1830, when Hugo was twenty-eight years old, he was a year late in turning in a manuscript to his publisher. Not only had he failed to complete the book, but he hadn't even begun it! He convinced his publisher to give him another six months. The deal was, if he didn't make this final deadline, he would have to return his significant advance to his publisher—money he needed to live on.

Hugo bought himself a bottle of ink and a pajama onesie made of wool and, to keep himself from going out of the house, he locked his other clothes away. Every night—all night—he wrote, leaving his room only to eat and sleep and to read drafts of the work to his friends. The harsh method worked—he actually turned his novel in a few weeks ahead of his deadline. The book he'd written, *The Hunchback of Notre-Dame*, made him world renowned! If you are someone who puts off important things till the last moment, you might get yourself a scratchy woolen onesie and lock *your* street clothes away.

My dad was a highly skilled procrastinator. He did his Christmas shopping on Christmas Eve and didn't begin his taxes till the evening of April 15, arriving at the post office in the nick of time! But other, more important things, like making the art he spent his life dreaming of making, he put off for so long that, after ninety-three years, death got to him first. Even if writing is at times overwhelming, don't let the thing that matters so much to you go undone forever.

Some of us use procrastination to our advantage. At times, it may have less to do with avoidance and more to do with the process of gestation—your poem may be nesting in your imagination. The poet Naomi Shihab Nye said, "I have always loved the gaps, the spaces between things. . . . I love staring, pondering, mulling. . . . Poetry calls us to pause."

Putting something off has the potential to fuel creativity. Thinking about your as-of-yet-unwritten poem, considering the images it will contain, can cause excitement to build. Tune in to yourself to determine whether you're pondering or evading your new poem.

When it comes to writing poems, keep in mind:

* There is no wrong way to write your poem.

* Trust your imagination.

* Play—don't take yourself too seriously.

* Remember that you don't have to share what you write with anyone unless you choose to.

* And most of all this: you'll feel better having written the words you tried so hard to avoid.

17 *And if You Don't Write?*

One morning when I was at my desk, the words kept rebuffing me. Not one that touched the paper was even close to what I wanted to say, and doubt gnawed at me as though I were its bone. "It's not like you're getting paid to be here," I said to myself, "so don't write."

I walked away from my notebook, feeling much relieved—I really didn't have to write, now did I? I took a deep breath and thought about what I'd do with the suddenly open hours. Until the impulse to write called me back. Apparently, it was going to be one of those days—damned if I did and damned if I didn't. Pushed to the edge, I relinquished control.

When I returned to the desk, here's what came:

If I don't write, I won't die. My eyes will still see
what they see, this heart, too. Blood won't stop
its pulse-work. Feet won't forget the forest is for
wandering through. Nor will I be less inclined
to comment on the world's beauty.

If I don't write, my imagination won't stop its
daily moment-by-moment insistence, not to make
something out of nothing, but to make a frog from a
prince, a window out of a wall, a day out of despair.

Without a pen in hand, a poem in mind,
phrases turned over in mind, my imagination
won't harden into the gray, flat matter of reason.
I won't forget to proclaim. Still, I'll be a diviner.

Or will I?

If I don't write, will I lose my way, give up my
song, forgetting its value—speech that for years I
begged for, clumsily stuttered toward, then thrust
my way into, and occasionally found waiting at my
doorstep, ready? If I don't write, will my imagina-
tion atrophy and, like an unused limb, dry up and
wither? Will a hard shell form around my ribcage,
a gnarled claw overtake my pen-holding hand?

Yes. If I don't write, my eyes will become
veiled and darkly hooded. Scales will bend my
back. My tongue will thicken into a knot that
not even the nimblest sailor will be able to untie.

And what if *you* don't write?

44

18   Losing Your Way, and Other Perils and Pitfalls

Do you remember the last time you got lost going someplace new and how that felt? For some of us, getting lost can be a complicated thing. Are we safe? Or are we experiencing new places that we'd have never found if we'd made all the correct turns?

More than once, walking alone in nature, I've taken a trail that didn't lead me where I thought it would, or the fog has been so thick, it has taken me a long time to find my way back. I've been lost in unfamiliar cities too. How about you? At such times, do you panic, or trust your reliable sense of direction to get you where you want to go?

Getting lost is hardly all bad. It gets us to notice the details of the environment because we're trying to figure out where we are and how to get back to a familiar place. At such times, we look for anything recognizable—a road sign, a tall building in the distance.

Then there's getting lost in writing. For me, it goes like this: there I was, happily scribbling away with a sense of direction and then poof, nothing.

Reading the last bit of what I've written can help me relocate myself, but not always. At such moments, the words that had muscle and beauty suddenly appear like nothing more than deflated balloons.

Just like when getting lost in a physical place, when you are lost in writing, take a few deep breaths and remind yourself that, eventually, you'll find your way. Past the corner of frustration and despair, you may find that you've actually ended up in a lush and beautiful place.

If not—if you feel deserted by your poem—it's a good time to take an actual walk in a familiar place and reclaim your spirit. Maybe put that poem away for a couple of days, or maybe, rejuvenated by the walk, you'll return to your notebook, ready to map a new way on paper.

46

19 *Abandoned on a Cold, Hard Street by Poetry: Writer's Block*

When you sit down to write and nothing comes, you may be experiencing writer's block. What you were about to write is now being kept from you under lock and key. You want to write and may have a vague sense of what's calling you to the page, but nothing is there. Zippo. It's as if a thick cement wall is between you and your writing, and that's a sad, frustrating feeling.

Safia Elhillo looks at writer's block this way: "I think writer's block is maybe a fear of writing a bad poem, and I am trying to stop being afraid of writing bad poems. A bad first draft now feels like a challenge instead of a failure. Or maybe it'll stay a bad poem, and that's okay, too—no one ever has to see it. But it lives on, for me, as evidence of a day I sat down to do my work anyway, to make something anyway."

Kim Addonizio seconds that when she says, "I try to let go of judgment and just be weird and put down whatever occurs to me; sometimes that helps me get unstuck. The biggest lesson I've learned is that I'm the one getting in my way. So, whatever you can do to get out of your own way and just do it, like Nike says . . . I mean the Nike who was the Greek goddess of victory. She was a war goddess. So, if you're battling some part of yourself that says, 'I can't, this is a waste of time,' and other self-defeating crap, she's good to have on your side."

Poet Sara Michas-Martin sees it this way: "At the root of writer's block (for me) is the question: *What do you need to be free from?* I think often writer's block is an extension of the ego. If we hold too tight to being *good* or *right*, we cage our creative spirit. What do you need in order to play and experiment without feeling tethered to a specific outcome?" Is there something that's caging your creative spirit, something you need to be free from?

Sometimes writers are afraid of telling. Maybe it's a story you were instructed to never repeat. Or maybe something happened to you that you pushed to the back of your mind because you didn't know how to make sense of it or it scared you too much. Getting close to writing something you're not ready to write can block you. If you're afraid to write something, that can be a fear worth respecting. Pushing ourselves to write what we're not ready to isn't the idea here. Your best writing won't come of that.

When you're ready to write those things, if you ever are, they'll be there. It's important not to write what you aren't ready to, and it's good to know when to push on ahead. Through writing, you'll develop the ability to discern between the two. Listen to your trustworthy inner voice and learn to distinguish between "yes" and "no."

Writing poems will serve you most if in the process of doing so you trust yourself. My experience as a writer has shown me that the memories that come to the fore of my heart and mind, especially those that persist, are those I'm both ready and able to write, even if it's hard, even if I stumble. If a poem is difficult to write, yet thoughts about it come to you repeatedly, it likely means you can handle it. But if you don't think so, then let that

poem go for another day or for always.

There may be poems that we don't feel up to the task of telling or we're doubtful of our ability to write. Experiment by writing the poem one way and then another. Poet Jericho Brown wrote of himself this way: "I am sick of your sadness, / Jericho Brown." Change your point of view; write in the second or third person. Play with the words. Let the story be light in your hands.

And remember, you can shred anything you want to. If you write something that you decide to throw away, you won't lose the experience of writing it; that is yours forever. However, if there's an experience that continues to knock at your door and you continue to turn it away, not writing it may become an impediment that keeps you from writing what will come afterward. Give space to what wants to be told.

Upon receiving the contract to write my first nonfiction book, *Writing and the Spiritual Life*, I was terrified. I'd convinced myself that the publisher had made a mistake in agreeing to publish my book—I'd never written much nonfiction before; poetry was my thing. The first couple of weeks of work, I was entirely and completely blocked.

Each morning, I'd get up, come to my desk with a strong coffee, stare at the blank document on my screen, and sweat. For hours. My heart was stuck in my throat, my mind was blank, my stomach knotted—I thought I'd throw up. Often that document would stay empty all morning. I'd go back to bed and shiver.

Sitting at my desk that late summer, after much cajoling and pleading with myself, and lots of patience, I finally wrote a sentence that I liked for its authenticity, for the way its words sounded in my mouth. It felt miraculous that in writing it I didn't die. That sounds silly now, but it's how I felt at the time. Knowing I'd set a difficult task for myself—to write a book linking writing with spirituality—I felt overwhelmed by the endeavor. For weeks, I regretted getting the thing I'd wanted most. But, you see, the publisher had sent me a check, and that check had helped to fund a trip to Europe. With the money gone, like Victor Hugo in his onesie, I had no choice but to write the book.

49

A few months into writing, after it had become, if not yet joyous (which it did become later), at least doable, I sent a few chapters to my editor. It took him forever to respond, and when he did, this is what came back: "Your writing is abstruse!" Yes, there was more to his letter, but that was its gist. I should have been offended. It should have caused the writing block to return, but that's not what happened.

Oddly, the editor's note made me happy because, I reasoned, only smart people could be abstruse—and here was an editor at a New York City publishing house telling me that I was. *So, darling*, I said to myself (not that I'd ever called myself "darling" before), *if he thought I was smart, it must be so.* Anytime you can look at a difficulty from another point of view, you can disarm it, and turn a writing block into sawdust!

If you've had to deal with frequent or recurrent criticism in your life, that criticism can get under the skin. This is another cause of writer's block. There's censorship from outside ourselves and also from within. If you want to write but think you're not good enough, you might be more susceptible to writer's block. However, you can refuse to succumb to such limitations.

50

The American poet William Stafford suggested to his students that when they felt blocked they should lower their expectations. He used a catch-as-catch-can method for writing. The story goes that early each morning, hours before he had to leave for his teaching job at the university, he'd get up, make himself a piece of dry toast and instant coffee (the poet in me would run the other way if offered such fare), and sit on his couch, the curtains open, with a notebook, watching daylight slowly overcome night.

Any word or idea that came to his mind, he'd accept and write down. Without judgment. With curiosity, faith, and belief. Poetry is everywhere and all the time, meaning it's available and not off-limits to you for any reason. That thinking will lead you to your greatest possibility.

When writing, remember to make a distinction between "bad" and "difficult." Just because the process of writing may sometimes be frustrating doesn't mean that the writing is bad, or that you are bad for wanting to write. Sometimes important things are difficult. That's the way it goes.

I've followed in Stafford's stead, and it's made all the difference in my writing life. A little something, a phrase no bigger than a walnut, is enough to get going. Even if what you start with gets edited out later, no matter; that's what got you going. It's like riding a bike—climb on and pedal and, once you pick up speed, you may end up in some pretty cool places. If we set the bar too high and have impossible expectations, we won't offer ourselves the most conducive mental and emotional environment for creativity. You want your imagination to prosper— feed it what it needs!

51

Another way to respond to being blocked is to make your own actual writer's block. Take a block of wood or plastic and paste small pictures you love on each of the six sides. Feel blocked and can't write? Toss that block like dice and begin writing in response to the image that appears on top.

The evening after receiving the first copy of *Writing and the Spiritual Life*, I slipped the book under my pillow. Late in the night, I woke up, turned on the light, and began looking through the pages, reading random words in a whisper, waking my husband.

"Babe, what are you doing?" "I'm reading words from my book." "Why are you doing that?" "To be sure none of them fell off the pages while I slept." By now he was fully awake. "That's impossible; they're printed on the paper."

"I'm glad you're convinced! But what if when you were doing the dinner dishes a few words fell into the soapy water?" "Impossible," he tried to reassure me. "Well, what if the dog ate some?"

"Babe, go back to sleep. We don't have a dog . . ."

Because writing that book had been a challenge, now that it was out, though I was proud of myself and so damn delighted—I'd come to love what I'd written—part of me was disbelieving. Turning away from Michael, I continued to check for missing words. He was right, there were none.

20   *Living with the Internal Critic*

One day in my early twenties when I was writing—or rather, one day when I was trying to write—a familiar feeling of withering came upon me, and daggers shot down each and every idea.

Finally, I'd had enough. I turned in my swivel chair to face the door. In a loud and angry voice I said, "Who are you? And what do you want from me?"

Suddenly I smelled cigarette smoke and heard the clickety-click of a woman's too-high high heels coming up the staircase outside. The back door opened. In walked a tall, thin woman wearing an Armani suit. She looked like my mother at her best.

With a hand on her hip, she stood facing me and asked, "Why do you continue to bother with something you're no good at?" She took a drag of her Chesterfield. "Really, you ought to do something useful! When was the last time you cleaned your oven?" she asked, opening its door and peering in. "And these windows! Now there's something that could benefit from your attention."

My shoulders bent forward and I felt myself shrinking when, as though suddenly inhabited by a force beyond myself, I stood up to my full five foot five, pointed a finger at her, and said, "Get out!" She looked at me and raised a well-plucked eyebrow. After I said "Get out" a second time, she turned on her heel and, in her clickety-click patent leathers, walked out. Oh, the imagination is a vast and vibrant place! And anger can be both livid and vivid. I'd finally had enough.

Need I say, nobody was actually there? Rather, that day, I manifested a feeling, personifying it into a being.

53

Those people who criticize you and whose voices you may have internalized over time are afraid that you'll look bad, make a mistake, or say something embarrassing. My internal critic (created over time by actual critics) was afraid I'd reveal the family secrets in my writing, and I have (again and again). That critic wasn't only my mother but an amalgam of both of my parents, as well as fierce Mother George from Catholic school and some of my teachers.

In a perverse sort of way, the critic wants to protect us. If we are kept small, and if we live, as it were, in a narrow box, then we won't make mistakes or say the wrong thing. We won't humiliate ourselves or our family. And it's awfully cozy in that box.

However, if you're stuck inside a box, you can't tell your vital truths.

Because you have gotten this far in this book, I'm pretty certain that box is too confining for you—it hasn't got even a single window from which to view the world, nor a door to walk through. And that won't do, not for you who has poems to write, things to say.

Here are a few suggestions for dealing with self-criticism:

* Imagine, like I did, that you can see your internal critic as separate from the rest of you. How does it look? Is it gendered? Does it wear high heels or Nikes? Is it even human? An animal, maybe, or an oddly formed, lumpy monster that smells bad?

One girl I worked with would see a guy who wore clothes too small for his big body and always smoked a stinky cigar. When she caught a whiff of that lit stogie, she knew her internal critic was back. Another student didn't see a figure but felt an oppressive weight overcome him.

* Drawing or writing about the critic will help you to personify it. I named mine Evelyn, pronounced "evil in." Once you envision the form of this part of yourself, it's easier to work with.

* Take your critic for a walk and tell it (nicely) to chill.

* Give your internal critic a job. "Wait till I'm done writing this poem and then help me punctuate it, would you?"

* Instruct your critic to leave the room, and be sure to close the curtains to prevent it from peering in the windows. Even if your critic is resistant at first, stay firm, and it will go.

The more you practice separating the critic from the essence of who you are, the more successful these processes will be. I'm proof in this regard that determination and persistence pay off. Which isn't to say that my critic doesn't ever show her coifed, hair-sprayed head, but when I hear her first steps, I respond before she can reduce me to nothing more than a puddle of frustration and fear.

Here's the deal: it's ultimately about what you believe. You can choose to believe in your inability (a regrettable choice, in my opinion). Or you can choose to believe in your imagination, your possibility, and the worthiness of your conviction. I used to find it easier to believe in my inability, but I'm done with that now! Sure, my writing needs support from others (I find a Grammar Queen helpful). By believing in my possibility, I make my writing stronger.

Lastly, if you don't have an internal critic, please don't make one up!

21   The Poet Within

You *may* have an internal critic but I'm certain there's a poet within you—otherwise, you wouldn't be writing poems.

No matter my age, the poet in me forever will be a girl about four years old. She's bright eyed, a little soft around the middle, wants to wear only dresses and shoes that don't crimp her feet, dances instead of walks, sings instead of talks.

She refuses to take "no" for an answer, is impulsive and enormously curious, and, just like most young children, she has an affinity for the question "Why?" because she wants to know almost everything. She's fearless—it's as easy for her to walk up onto a stage as into a dark forest. The stars, she's told me, are her cousins. There's often dirt underneath her fingernails and either a broad smile across her face or fast, furious tears running down it. She doesn't know shame or false pride. This girl is my cheerleader-defender all in one, and no matter how heavy *my* baggage, she travels light.

56

As with the internal critic, you'll gain clarity and strength from imagining your own poet within. On a day when inspiration is slow to come or self-doubt burdens you, when you've listened to someone say unkind things about your poems (or any other part of you) and you feel yourself giving in to that belief, get a picture in your head of your very own poet and watch that negativity slink away.

When I first envisioned my poet within, I got out my watercolors and painted a smiling girl in a pink dress. In every home I've had since then, she's stood near my writing place, watching over me.

Maybe watercolors will be your way to flesh out your poet. A hunk of clay? A song? Words on the page? Don't rush. You're not making something up; you're discovering what's already there.

Here are things to consider when envisioning your poet within (keep in mind, some of these may apply to *your* poet while others may not):

* Does your poet have a human form or might it be from another universe entirely?
* Does it have a superpower or more than one?
* What's the sound of your poet's voice?

* How does it let you know of its presence?

PART II

"If One Part Were Touched,
the Whole Would Tremble":
Writing Poetry
from the Inside Out

This section will give you an in-depth look at poetry's components.

22   *Loving Words*

The Spanish poet Federico García Lorca's poem "Romance Sonambulo" starts off "Verde que te quiero verde" ("Green, how I love you, green"). In Spanish, the verb "to want" can also mean "to love." What words would you go so far as to declare love for?

Is it a word's meaning or its sound that woos you? Maybe it's the way the word feels in your mouth when you speak it. Some words are smooth. Others are ice that won't melt. Certain words inflame me; I want to spit them out. Some words hiss; others stammer. Some tell truths we're not able to hear.

Here are words that I love for their uplift: "stream," "oh," "dandelion," "tomorrow." "Stream" because right now it's pouring outside the cabin where I'm staying in the near middle of nowhere, and the stream is running fast, taking with it every dubious thought I have. "Oh" is for my husband saying "Oh, baby" to me—how it sounds *and* what it means. "Tomorrow" is for my tendency to look ahead with glee, and "dandelion" because its yellowness says spring.

You might like to make word lists on your rainy days and pull them out when your vocabulary feels tinny to the ear. List every word you want in your life—those you crave for their meaning, their sound, how they look on the page.

Take the onomatopoeic word "perplex" that stops the tongue at the wall of "per" and again at "pl," finally hitting hard against that last "x." As one who is frequently perplexed, I love the word, but it's not one I'm going to walk around with in my mouth and ears all day, as it would make me question too many things. But the wet ease and forward movement of the word "river" is calming.

At night, when I can't sleep, I follow the technique that Patti Smith wrote about in her book *Devotion (Why I Write)*. I'll choose a letter of the alphabet and say all the words beginning with that letter that I can think of. Next thing I know, it's morning.

Back when poetry first called my name, many of my poems had the word "gather" in them, in an effort to contain my un-gatherable self. Now I recoil at that word. It's become so commonplace in advertisements for the food and restaurant world. I'd prefer to gather flowers in my backyard garden.

Begin to notice the language you're drawn to, the words you respond to upon hearing or reading them, those that repeat in your poems, and the ones you want to invite into your writing. The novelist Hortense Calisher said, "The words! I collected them in all shapes and sizes and hung them like bangles in my mind." Yes, do that.

23   What Makes a Poem a Poem?

The simplest (and my favorite) definition of a poem is "a picture made out of words." It's a picture of an instant in time, a memory, the sketch of a person, animal, or place, a true or invented occurrence, the moment of change.

Through the use of images—things that can be seen, smelled, tasted, touched, or heard—poets turn thoughts and feelings into poems. Those word pictures may show us what we don't expect to see and may take us to places we might otherwise never visit.

A poem can't recreate an experience—that's already come and gone. Rather, a poem becomes a new thing. The event is what made you reach for pen and paper or phone.

First there's what happened, either something in "real" life or in your imagination, your heart.

Writing your poem is the *second* thing. Through the process of writing, that magical, unpredictable experience of alchemy, the bare bones of what occurred and what you were feeling about it shifts and deepens. You may discover that it's connected to other experiences, and those may enter the poem also.

The *third* thing is the poem itself. Instead of being a retelling of what happened, it will be its own thing, *your* own thing, comprising who you are and who you were and, maybe, who you will be.

There is no subject that a poem can't touch. Nothing is too small or large or unimportant. Remember this: what comes to you is what is there for you to write. In poetry, there's never one right answer, never only one way to describe anything—from a slap across the face to the view from a mountaintop.

Most poems contain a rather small collection of words—images, phrases, sentences. You can hold a poem under your tongue or slip one into your pocket. Short on words, however, doesn't imply light on meaning. In a poem, every word carries weight.

A poem can express the inexpressible. A ten-line poem may boomerang in your heart for days. It may change how you see yourself or how you understand the world. Take this one by Rumi, the Persian poet born over eight hundred years ago in what is now Afghanistan:

64

> *We are walking through a garden.*
> *I turn away for a minute.*
> *You're doing it again.*
> *You have my face here, but you look at flowers!*

Feel the poet's grief? It only takes Rumi two lines to set the scene and only two more to make us sad. You know what it's like to be ignored, don't you? Poetry gets to the essential, and quickly!

The nineteenth-century American poet Emily Dickinson said, "I hesitate which word to take, as I can take but few and each must be the chiefest." Because a poem is made of condensed language, each word counts. Which are your "chiefest" words?

However, as true as Dickinson's statement is, in the first drafts welcome every word that comes. Don't pick over them like fruit in a basket. Later, in final drafts, you'll need to decide which words are the best ones and keep only those, but at first accept them all.

Poetry relies on concrete language, not abstraction. If Rumi had written, "She doesn't love me anymore," you might not believe him. The poet shows us what he feels through describing the actual world.

Poems recognize life's small gestures and draw readers to notice things that, if the poem hadn't been written, likely would have gone unremarked upon—the delicate drift of a downward falling leaf, a face searching for yours across a crowded room—and show them to us in new ways.

The English poet Eleanor Farjeon, born in 1881, wrote:

> *The tide in the river runs deep.*
> > *I saw a shiver*
> > *Pass over the river*
> *As the tide turned in its sleep.*

Until reading her poem, I'd have never thought of a river sleeping. And can't you picture that "shiver" as the tide changed?

Farjeon's poem leaves a lot out. She doesn't tell us what trees grow alongside the water. Nor does she indicate who is observing the scene. Poems never say everything; they always leave something out. A poem's job is not to tell you how to get to the corner of Sunset Avenue and Fourteenth Street. The poem wants to give you a sense of standing at that windy corner. By leaving parts of the story out, the poem invites the reader in.

If a poem were a simple mathematical equation, it wouldn't be $1 + 1 = 2$; it would be butterfly + mountain = the first moment I saw you. A poem often takes leaps like Superman, "able to leap tall buildings in a single bound." Not everything is explained but somehow the poem isn't missing anything. That is its integrity.

A poem can allow the speechless to speak. In her poem "to the sea," Aracelis Girmay writes:

> *How dare I move into the dark space of your body*
> *carrying my dreams, without an invitation . . .*

The ocean can't literally invite her into its water,
but Girmay imagines it could. That's one way a poem
enlarges our understanding of the world, by making it
possible for us to see differently.

Sound is an important and unique element to poetry.
But for now, keep in mind that, though not all poems
rhyme, the element of sound is nearly always at work.
Sometimes it's quite obvious, like the beat of a drum,
while in other poems, it's subtle as the beat of your heart
at rest.

Both when writing and when reading a poem, though
your body may be still, you begin in one place and end
up in another.

24 *The Various Forms Poetry Takes: From Free Verse to the Villanelle*

Most poetry that's published these days is written in
what's called "free verse." These poems don't follow
a formal form. Without rhyme or repetitive meter,
the direction the poem takes isn't controlled by a
predetermined pattern. Often poets create their own
structures for their poems—a particular poem might
be written in couplets, or the poet may repeat a single
phrase for emphasis.

Sometimes "free verse" gets confused with "blank
verse," which is not at all the same. Blank verse is
unrhymed poetry written in iambic pentameter, the
most traditional meter, with lines of ten syllables each,

in which an unstressed syllable is followed by a stressed one. Iambic pentameter rhythm is akin to the da-**dum** of the heart, making it not only predictable but familiar and comforting. Here are two examples (the stressed syllables are in bold): From *Twelfth Night*, by Shakespeare, "If **mu**sic **be** the **food** of **love**, play **on**"; and from John Donne's "Holy Sonnet XIV," "Your **force** to **break**, blow, **burn**, and **make** me **new**."

There are many types of poetry. You're likely familiar with haiku, a form originating in Japan that has only three lines (five syllables in the first and third line and seven in the second). I'll bet you wrote at least one haiku at some point in school. Other forms may be new to you. The ode is a poem written in dedication to someone or something. An elegy is a poem written upon a loved one's death in which the beloved is remembered and celebrated. Perhaps you're familiar with the sonnet, a fourteen-line love poem that originated in thirteenth-century Italy. Two highly structured forms that are popular these days are the sestina and the villanelle. In the third section of the book, we'll look at the ghazal, a very old form that comes from seventh-century Arabia.

Striving to fit into a precise form is actually expansive; you'll write in ways you wouldn't naturally be inclined to.

25   *The Element of Sound*

"Poems are a form of music, and language just happens to be our instrument—language and breath," says the poet Terrance Hayes. Whether it rhymes or not, sound is more intrinsic to poetry than it is to any other written form, except for songs.

Remember learning the ABC song when you were little? When rhythm and/or rhyme is added to what's said, it makes the information easier to remember.

Meaning doesn't just come through a word's definition but through the sounds the word makes. Take the sound of the word "please," how it eases into the ear, asking.

To give a sense of how sound works, let's look at excerpts from two very different poems. "Speech to the Young: Speech to the Progress-Toward," was written by Gwendolyn Brooks, an American poet born in 1917, who began publishing her work when she was only thirteen years old. The poem begins:

> *Say to them,*
> *say to the down-keepers,*
> *the sun-slappers,*
> *the self-soilers,*
> *the harmony-hushers*

This punctuative, declarative poem is like a chant. Brooks's staccato keeps the poem moving at a brisk clip.

"Rock Me to Sleep," by poet Elizabeth Akers Allen, was written in the 1880s. It relies on end rhymes, as was typical of poetry then:

> *Backward, turn backward, O Time, in your flight,*
> *Make me a child again just for tonight!*
> *Mother, come back from the echoless shore,*
> *Take me again to your heart as of yore*

With its rhythm, made up in part of the vowel
sounds—the repeated "o" sound, and the pleading of the
long "i"—this poem conveys a sense of longing.

Years ago, at a retreat center by the Pacific Ocean in
Washington, I participated in a weeklong writing work-
shop led by Mary Oliver. What stuck with me most was
what she taught us about the element of sound in poetry.

"Say the word 'rock,'" she instructed, "and then say
'stone.'" "Rock" sounds rigid. We know "stone" to be a
hard thing, but with the softness of the "s," the openness
of the "o" and "n," the word itself conveys softness.

Oliver went on to list word ending sounds that stop
readers, at least as much as punctuation will, and those
that effortlessly lead a reader into what comes next.
Only a few ending sounds halt us in our tracks. "B," "d,"
"g," "k," "p," "r," and "t" will cause the reader to stop
abruptly. This is true whether we're reading to ourselves
or aloud.

Look at these three lines from the poem "etymology,"
about her first name, by Airea D. Matthews:

my "e" is silent

like most people should be   *the consonant is sonorant*

      is a Black woman   *or one might say the spine*

The last word of the first line—"silent"—stops us, doesn't

pull us into the next line quickly, so that when we get to "like most people should be" we've had a moment to get ready. Again, in the next line, the abruptness of "t" slows our reading. The following line, though, ends softly, with the word "spine" pulling us along.

Ultimately, everything about a poem—line length, sound, punctuation, tone, and syntax—supports its meaning. And the unique way in which each poet puts these things together makes up a writer's style.

Here are a few brief definitions of aspects of sound in poetry that you might want to experiment with:

RHYME, HALF RHYME, AND INTERNAL RHYME

* Rhyme is when the ending sound repeats. From William Blake's "The Tyger":

> *Tyger Tyger, burning **bright**,*
> *In the forests of the **night***

And from Elizabeth Bishop's poem "Sonnet," which she wrote when she was just seventeen:

> *With melody, deep, clear, and liquid-**slow**.*
> *Oh, for the healing swaying, old and **low***

* Half rhyme is when the ending sound almost rhymes, but not quite. Some years back, the musician Eminem was able to rhyme the word "orange" with "door hinge" and "four-inch," partly because of how he accented the words.

In Yeats's poem "Lines Written in Dejection," he says,

> *When have I last looked **on***
> *The round green eyes and the long wavering bodies*
> *Of the dark leopards of the **moon?***

* Internal rhyme is when a word within a line rhymes
with a word within or at the end of another line. Many
poems with internal rhyme also use ending rhyme.
From Edgar Allan Poe's "Annabel Lee":

> *For the moon never beams, without bringing me dreams*
> *   Of the beautiful Annabel Lee;*
> *And the stars never rise but I feel the bright eyes*
> *   Of the beautiful Annabel Lee*

Rhyme, rhythm, and meter help us to learn poems by
heart and contribute to the music of a poem.

RHYTHM AND METER

The various kinds of meter hold in common a pattern of
sound—the repetition of particular groups of syllables.
Some syllables are stressed while others are quiet.

In iambic pentameter, the most common meter,
which resembles the sound pattern of the heartbeat, the
first syllable is unaccented and the second is accented.
"Come **live** with **me** and **be** my **love**," wrote Christopher
Marlowe. And from Shakespeare: "Shall **I** com**pare** thee
to a **sum**mer's **day**?"

Read these lines aloud and notice the subtlety of

sound, how your voice moves from down to up. Because your voice is quieter in the first syllable, the accented second sound is reinforced.

Whether or not you choose to rhyme your poems, or to write in formal meter, tuning your ears to how sound works in poetry will make your poems stronger.

26   *The Shape of It*

You with your beautiful body and the world of human beings with theirs are hardly the only ones for whom shape matters. Expand the definition of "being" to include poems, and note how poems can also be wide or narrow, angular or rounded.

Most poems appear as lines on the page. The length of a line contributes to the meaning of that line, and to the meaning of the entire poem. This is unique to poetry—prose doesn't offer readers sculptural shape. In poetry, the place where the line ends is called the "line break."

Read a particularly angular poem that's got only one or two words on each line and you'll notice there's a lot of white space on either side of the poem, so whatever appears on the line, whether it's as insignificant as "the" or as striking as "fire," is going to get a lot of attention standing all alone in the middle of the page. Consider this when deciding how to shape your poems—does any single word in the poem require that kind of priority? This is usually decided in the later drafts of a poem, because we've got to be well inside the poem in order to know.

Let's look at one sentence, near the middle of Jenny Xie's poem "Naturalization":

The years are slow to pass, heavy footed.

73

What if she'd broken it this way:

The years are slow
to pass, heavy
footed.

We wouldn't know what about the years is slow till we got to the next line, nor would we know in what way they were heavy, which would create a very different effect. By giving us the sentence in a single line, Xie tells us that she wants to convey this material all at once, not bit by bit.

No matter how many words appear on a line, the two words that will receive the most attention are the line's first word and, especially, its last. A line's final word is what a reader is left with, even for the fraction of a second it takes for the eye and mind to travel to the beginning of the next line.

The most traditional approach is for a line to contain a single phrase or sentence, giving a reader enough content to be momentarily satisfied. If a poet wants to pull a reader quickly through their poem they may end a line in the middle of a thought with a word that ends softly. If a poet wants to unsteady a reader, they may end a line in an entirely unexpected place, almost defying the line itself, and in those cases, they may choose words that have hard ending sounds, to create a jarring effect. Let's look at a few examples.

Robert Louis Stevenson begins "Bed in Summer" this way:

74

> *In winter I get up at night*
> *And dress by yellow candle-light.*

The first line ends with certainty. Stevenson has given us a phrase, enough to satisfy, ending the line with a hard-sounding word. The next line completes the sentence. (Note that the second line, which is not a new sentence, begins with a capitalized word. This is old-school. Plenty of contemporary poets do it too. It's a personal choice. As I see it, a line beginning with a capital letter that *doesn't* begin a sentence keeps me from moving easily into the next phrase. In my own work, I only capitalize the first word of a line if it also begins a new sentence.)

In the opening to Margarita Engle's "Turtle Came to See Me," she both ends lines at the conclusion of phrases and breaks this pattern:

> *The first story I ever write*
> *is a bright crayon picture*
> *of a dancing tree, the branches*
> *tossed by island wind.*

The first two lines give us almost enough content to be

satisfied, but not quite; Engle is pulling us into her poem. That third line, though, because there's no verb in it, makes us wonder about the branches. She's urging us onward.

Here's "A Strange Beautiful Woman" by Marilyn Nelson:

> *A strange beautiful woman*
> *met me in the mirror*
> *the other night,*
> *Hey,*
> *I said,*
> *What you doing here?*
> *She asked me*
> *the same thing.*

Take a look at the fourth and fifth lines. Nelson wants to slow us down, to get us to pay attention. In most poems, the words "I said" wouldn't warrant standing alone on a single line because those words are generally only segues to further content, but here Nelson is using the words as a single line to let us know something's going on that we should take notice of.

In addition to how an individual line conveys content, there is what the stanza does. A stanza—a unit of lines—is akin to a paragraph in prose. Stanzas signify a separation, a transition, letting the reader know that something a bit different is happening. It could be that each stanza offers a particular point of view. Two-line stanzas are called couplets, three-line stanzas are tercets, and four-line stanzas are quatrains.

The best way to get familiar with how to use line and

stanza breaks is to experiment. Take a line in a poem you're working on and break it in multiple ways, and notice how you influence the meaning by doing so. Do this with stanzas also. Or take someone else's poem— maybe a favorite published poem—and see what happens when you break the lines differently from the way the poet did. I'll bet by doing so you'll discover why the poet did what she did. And, of course, as with all aspects of acquainting yourself with poetry, read, read, read, and see how lots of other poets handle lines and stanzas.

27   *To Punctuate or Not to Punctuate*

Another thing I learned from Mary Oliver that has stayed with me comes from the one-on-one session we had. She'd read a handful of my poems and, noticing my inconsistent use of punctuation, suggested that I pick—either punctuate a poem correctly and completely, or don't use any punctuation at all. In a kind way, Oliver was pointing out that my inconsistent use of punctuation reflected a lack of clarity of thought, and she was right.

Poets each find their own way to this, and the way punctuation is used may depend on the poem. In some of his work, W. S. Merwin used neither punctuation nor capital letters, and his line breaks appear design influenced—those poems look block-like on the page—rather than content determined. He punctuated other poems in a customary way.

Here's the opening of his poem "Rain Light." Though

Merwin uses no punctuation and his only capital letter is
the one that starts the poem off, as you begin to read, it's
clear that nearly each line is a sentence:

> *All day the stars watch from long ago*
> *my mother said I am going now*
> *when you are alone you will be all right*
> *whether or not you know you will know*

In some of his work, though, it's not at all obvious
where one sentence ends and the next begins. A few
readings are needed to figure out where a new thought
starts. Take the opening to "End of a Day":

> *In the long evening of April through the cool light*
> *Bayle's two sheep dogs sail down the lane like magpies*
> *for the flock a moment before he appears near the oaks*
> *a stub of a man rolling as he approaches*
> *smiling and smiling and his dogs are afraid of him*

Consider punctuation, like line and stanza breaks, as
directions you provide to guide the reader, indicating,
"Slow down a little here" (with a comma); "Stay a bit
longer here" (with a period); "Let's hang out for a
moment" (with a stanza break). The reader wants to
know he can trust you, so tell him what you want him to
do. Or you can, like Merwin, make a reader work to find
their way, allowing not only for potential confusion but
for discovery.

28   *Voice and Style*

The elements of **voice** and **style** are very closely
connected and, like cracks in the sidewalk, they've
always tripped me up. If they baffle you, too, don't feel
bad. Defined simply, **style** equals **diction** (word choice),
and **tone**. Both convey the writer's attitude toward their
subject. Each writer has their own **voice**; it's what makes
the writing uniquely theirs. Now for a closer look.

Here are the opening two lines of two very differ-
ent poems that begin in *almost* the same way. First is
"Daughter," by Jon Pineda:

> *Let us take the river*
> *path near Fall Hill.*

Next is "OK Let's Go," by Maureen N. McLane:

> *Let's go to Dawn School*
> *and learn again to begin*

Though small, the difference between "Let us" and
"Let's" is distinctive—"Let us" is formal, whereas "Let's"
is relaxed. It's *style* that allows Pineda and McLane to
each convey their own sensibility and tone. And then
there's the informal tone of McLane's "OK."

Some poets write in an ornate style. Others have a
straightforward approach. Some build a poem from
simple, single-phrase sentences; while others write entire
poems consisting of one long, complex, twisting and

78

turning sentence. The way a poet designs their poems on the page—their actual appearance—also contributes to their style. Attitude toward a subject is conveyed through both word choice and tone. Respect or disrespect toward a subject will determine a writer's word choices. The style of a particular piece of writing is also determined, in later drafts, by consideration of the intended audience.

A poet's voice is the written manifestation of their personality. How you will say things is unique to who you are. Through writing (and writing), poets refine and expand their unique way of expressing themselves. In his book *The Art of Voice*, Tony Hoagland says, "The role of voice in poetry is to deliver the paradoxical facts of life with warmth and élan, humor, intelligence, and wildness."

Our poetry voices are based on the voices we've heard during our lives, as well as how language is used in the places we've come from—including sounds other than human voices, such as city background sounds or those of the ocean. Were you read to as a child? Did someone tell you stories? Those will influence your poet's voice too. My mother read me poetry every day from the time I was a baby, and though my poems are nothing like A. A. Milne's children's poems, the rhythm of his work is present in my own.

Tony Hoagland said, "Whatever the 'matter' of a poem is, it is carried along on the fluid tide of a voice." It is not only poets' different content that makes their work identifiable to you, but the way their voices handle that content—a kind of signature, as unique to them as their dreams and fingerprints. The *way* they write about their content is their *voice*.

Both Frank O'Hara's poetry voice and style are conversational. He wrote in a way that conveys a friendliness and accessibility. When I read O'Hara's poems it's as though he's in the room talking to me. Take the opening lines, the first stanza, to his poem "Animals":

80

> *Have you forgotten what we were like then*
> *when we were still first rate*
> *and the day came fat with an apple in its mouth*

"Have you forgotten" implies we once shared something together, and even though we're his readers and not his friends, his language brings us in. O'Hara's tone and attitude come through in his anticipation, as though he were preparing for the feast of his life. Style and voice are interwoven and worth looking at closely because understanding them will help you as you discover the way in which you'll write your poems.

29 "Since Feeling Is First": The Troublesome Adjective and Getting to Original Thought

E. E. Cummings wrote a poem called "Since feeling is first," and as the author of nearly three thousand poems, he ought to know. The poem begins this way:

since feeling is first
who pays attention
to the syntax of things
will never wholly kiss you;
. . . .
and kisses are a better fate
than wisdom

Feeling is often first; it's poetry's turf. Much creative writing begins out of a shift in feeling—unsettled or suddenly elated, we reach for a scrap of paper.

Typically, when asked, "How are you?" we respond by saying, "Fine." But what is fine? All that response will commit to is being positive, and it's not necessarily honest (but convenient, yes). Saying "fine" may also be a way to avoid saying what's true, if you don't want to reveal that, at the moment, you're falling apart.

What if, when asked, "How are you?" you answered, "A little blue around the edges but sugary once you get deeper in," or "Spicy. Today, I'm enough to burn your tongue!"

The limitedness of "fine" doesn't belong to that word alone. Other abstract adjectives such as "nice," "pretty," and "wonderful" aren't actually nice, pretty, or wonderful. They're vague and, in poetry, leave too much up to the interpretation of a reader. When a poem requires a reader to read it a few times, it should be to understand the poem's complexity, not to try to decipher its meaning because the poet hasn't done his job. The use of abstract adjectives conveys a lack of conviction, indicating that the poet is unsure of what he's saying, and that means that the poem isn't finished.

By the time you get to a final draft, you need to convey an integrity of meaning in your poem. The poem needs to show why you think and feel as you do. Are you enamored of a guy because of how well he listens when you share something important? Is he calm when you get ruffled, patient when you're ill-tempered?

I could tell you that my friend is nice because (sometimes) she is, or I could tell you that the winter sunrise this morning was nice because it was. My friend, however, doesn't turn pink and orange and come up at morning, and the sunrise doesn't laugh the way that girl does. Ntozake Shange, most famously the author of the choreopoem *for colored girls who have considered suicide / when the rainbow is enuf*, said, "A poem should happen to you like cold water or a kiss." Feel how physical and unequivocal, how not abstract, that is.

Consider these lines by the Chilean poet Pablo Neruda, from his love poem "Sonnet Eleven." When Neruda writes, "the liquid measure of your steps," can't you see the smooth ease of movement? And when he says, "I hunger for your sleek laugh," have you ever thought of a laugh as being sleek? I hadn't. In describing his love, Neruda says, "the sovereign nose of your arrogant face," making the reader see a proud rather than boastful woman.

When using adjectives, choose sensory ones that you can see, hear, smell, touch, or taste—ones that live in the body. Embrace words like "tall," "jagged," "ripe," "bitter," "acrid," "toothsome," "creamy," "blurred," "prickly," "solid," "smooth," "elastic," "rough." If you're going to use adjectives—and you will—make them unpredictable and as specific as possible.

There is one caveat when it comes to the abstract adjective: in life, if someone you love says, "Hello, gorgeous," that's a good thing. Maybe don't ask that person to be more specific.

30   Simile and Metaphor

Poets use similes and metaphors to express their point of view and to give clarity and depth to an image, experience, emotion, or idea. Both techniques compare two dissimilar things by showing readers often-surprising ways in which they're alike.

Léopold Senghor was both a poet and the first president of Senegal. In his poem "I Want to Say Her Name" he personified features of Africa that he loved, writing:

> *Naëtt, her name has the sugared whiteness of coffee trees*
> *   in flower*
> *It's the savannah which blazes . . .*
> *Naëtt, it's the dry whirlwind and the dense clap of*
> *   thunder.*

In "Poems for Blok," the twentieth-century Russian poet Maria Tsvetaeva wrote a poem to her poet friend Alexander Blok:

> *Your name is a—bird in my hand*
> *a piece of ice on my tongue . . .*
> *A ball caught in flight,*
> *a silver bell in my mouth . . .*

How much there can be in a name! We know that a name doesn't literally have sugared whiteness, nor can a name be a silver bell. But, by making these leaps, both poets articulate their feelings—Senghor for his continent and Tsvetaeva for her friend.

Similes, as you likely learned in grade school, most often use the words "like" or "as" (or, less commonly, "than" or "as if") to bridge the two parts of the sentence. The metaphor does away entirely with the bridge and takes a leap, saying this *is* that.

This poem fragment by the ancient Greek poet Sappho is made up of only a single simile. By showing us wind through a tree, Sappho demonstrates what's happened to her heart:

> *Without warning,*
> *as a whirlwind*
> *swoops on an oak*
> *love shakes my heart.*

Having been awakened from a nap on a hot day by the sound of someone walking into his room wearing tinkling ankle bracelets, Michael Ondaatje wrote an ironically titled poem, "Sweet Like a Crow." It begins:

> *Your voice sounds like a scorpion being pushed*
> *through a glass tube*
> *like someone has just trod on a peacock*
> *like wind howling in a coconut*
> *like a rusty bible . . .*

Next time you or I are woken from a nap, may it have poetic consequences!

In her poem "Dear America," Rachel Eliza Griffiths uses both metaphor and simile in a single sentence:

> *Your alphabet wraps itself*
> *like a tourniquet*
> *around my tongue.*

An alphabet can't literally wrap itself around something, nor is it actually a tourniquet that cuts off circulation, but Griffiths wants to demonstrate the power that one particular alphabet has over her.

In his poem "Love in the Ruins," Jim Moore uses the words "as if" to connect something common with something of great importance, describing his mother

> *folding the tablecloth after dinner*
> *so carefully,*
> *as if it were the flag*
> *   of a country that no longer existed,*
> *but once had ruled the world.*

That's some folding. Feel the care she gives her task, leaving the reader with a weight of sadness?

Experiment with this: spend a day writing similes and metaphors unconnected to poems. Make a bank of them—some that, at first glance, are wild and unconnected—to draw from later. Including figurative language is another way to draw your readers in.

31   By Heart or By Head

Along with reading and writing poems—and living life, and staying aware of what's around you so that you can respond—memorizing poems will support your writing greatly. Once you no longer need to look at the words on the page, you'll be able to fully enter and get to know a poem. And that will allow you to hear and feel what it most intimately says.

To say a poem out loud gives the words far greater power than when they rest silently on paper. Memorize a poem and make it yours, and you can stand beside any of your favorite poets, from Elizabeth Acevedo to Emily Dickinson. With a few poems under your belt, you'll never be bored or lonely again! Those poems will keep you company when you're waiting in line for coffee. You'll be a great asset to any party—if the conversation lags, recite a couple of poems and the room will become lively again as listeners respond.

We talk of this as "learning by heart," but one evening, after reciting several poems to my friend Cheryl's grandkids, her grandson Sami asked, "Do you know any more poems by head?" Luckily, I did. We use our heads to fasten the poems securely to our hearts.

Here are some suggestions for learning poems by heart (and by head):

* Only memorize a poem you love.

* Begin with a short poem.

* Silently read the poem over a few times, getting to
know it.

* Next read it aloud a few times and begin to lift your
eyes from the page. Memorize the poem phrase by
phrase, then sentence by sentence.

* Notice clues within the poem that will aid your
memory, such as end rhymes or content or sound
repetition—perhaps an "m" sound that you hear over
and over. Use the content to help you remember. If
something in the poem reminds you of an experience
you've had, that will make memorizing it easier.

In the final section of this book we'll talk about reading
poems aloud and performing them. This is a good place
to start.

32 *Where Do You Write?*

The best room of my own was the third-floor San
Francisco studio at the corner of Larkin and Union
where I lived by myself for a year when I was in my
early twenties. In a corner of the room, atop my father's
drawing table, in front of the three big windows, sat my
electric Smith Corona typewriter. It was the first thing I
saw upon waking each morning.

Now my office is a bedroom in our small two-bedroom
house on a nondescript, quiet street in Monterey. I love

this room not so much for the window that looks out at a Monterey pine tree, but because when I'm there, the cats, Ace and Stella, usually join me, and any place is made better by their whiskered presence. (The poet William S. Burroughs said, "My relationship with my cats has saved me from a deadly, pervasive ignorance," and I concur.)

In my office there's a long narrow desk that my husband built for me, and more books than bookshelves; the un-shelved books form disordered columns on the floor. It's been said, "Creative minds are rarely tidy," and I agree—neither my mind nor my room could be described as tidy. The desk is often covered with piles of papers. I think the external chaos is a manifestation of the chaos in my head, and that's oddly calming.

In addition to the cats, I keep certain objects around me that hold meaning. There's a large yellow and red Guatemalan painted box that serves as an altar to creativity. Atop it sits a photo of the fox who once spent a weekend in my backyard, a photo of my mother before she was wrung out, a rough garnet crystal that I found in a nearby wood, and a note from a former second-grade student, which reads, "Pictures just come to my mind, and I tell my heart to go ahead."

Novelist Rachel Kushner says, "I know that things bear mystical emanations. . . . I'm particular about what things are allowed in. Only those that glow with some kind of special meaning." It comforts me to know that other writers also surround themselves with objects that function as talismans to support their writing.

If you don't have a room of your own in which to work, where will you write? Poet Paul Muldoon says, "I've now made a virtue of necessity and am committed to the idea of the workspace as pop-up." He writes at the dining room table, "which I now reconfigure each day in the hope of doing a little divining." Divining—now that's a great word to describe what poets do. At day's end, the poet clears the table so the evening meal may be enjoyed there.

Safia Elhillo tells me, "I spend most of my life traveling . . . so I don't have a favorite location to write, though I would love to have one someday—a favorite café or a real desk. . . . Mostly I write in bed, wherever I am. And I like writing on the Amtrak, too—the tray tables are almost the perfect height." Kim Addonizio says, "Mostly I write on the couch or in bed, where I feel far away from the world and things."

If you have your own bedroom, you might turn a corner of it into your writing space and adorn it with items of significance. If you don't have a room that's yours, like Paul Muldoon, create pop-up workstations, or write in bed or in the stacks at your local library. You might bring a small object that glows with you, or perhaps your dog will curl up at your feet.

33   Tools of the Trade

Though a lot of *you* is required to write a poem, not a lot of materials are needed. Writing is a portable art form—stuff a notebook and a pencil in your backpack, or pull out your tablet, and you're good to go.

When working on a screen, keep your drafts so that you can go back to them. I often reclaim parts of early versions. You might find the perfect word or phrase there.

I've found that the tools I use can influence what I write. When writing poems, I tend to begin with pen and paper and to write the first couple of drafts by hand. The physical sensation of holding the pen and moving it across the paper: the nub of it, paper absorbing ink, the fluidity of my horrible handwriting, smooth and *slow*, except when a thought comes quickly and my pen scrambles to catch it all. After that, I'm back to slow—a pace I'm rather fond of and don't have enough of in most parts of my life. Once I've got a solid paper draft, I reread it and go to the computer, where, as I type the material, it begins to take final form.

Writing prose tends to begin, for me, at the computer. Because of its greater linearity and the speed at which my initial thoughts tend to come, having the keyboard beneath my fingers works best. But to begin a poem that way would be a bit like broadcasting news before the story's happened.

When I was in middle school, my mother insisted I learn the keyboard. If all else failed, she was determined that I'd have typing as a skill to fall back on. It's one that helped keep her employed as a secretary throughout her working life. She could type something like 183 words per minute with maybe only a couple of mistakes. A few hours every day of one terribly long summer were spent before my mother's IBM Selectric typewriter. I wasn't a happy girl; my friends were at the beach while I was stuck indoors stumbling before a humming machine. I can't type 183 words per minute, but thanks to her, I'm pretty fast!

The notebook—we've got to talk about the notebook. You need one (or several). It doesn't matter what kind. I personalize mine, often with a collage on the front. On the inside covers I write quotes that I find encouraging so that when I'm on the verge of frustration, I read one and am revived.

When I asked the poet Sara Michas-Martin for her suggestions to new writers, she responded, "Keep a notebook with you. Draw in it. Write down things people say, lines from books that grab your attention, and observations about the world."

I also keep what I call Another Notebook nearby, to jot down ideas that don't immediately fit in with what I'm writing but that I want to keep for possible later use.

34: Rules You'll Love to Follow: A Surprising List

These may be the best rules you're ever given, though it's likely they won't be the easiest to follow. Initially, I made this list, bit by bit, for myself, and I have scoffed at it upon occasion; but I keep coming back because it works.

#1. What you write doesn't have to make sense. Let yourself be foolish.

"What you write doesn't have to make sense" is not to

suggest that you write a random collection of words as though they'd fallen out of your pocket, and there you are scooping them up from the sidewalk before the wind takes them. But it's also *not* to suggest that you don't do that. Sense will come; there's no need to hurry to get there.

#2. Trust your imagination. Creative writing goes beyond mere intellect; trust your imaginative abilities.

#3. Don't plan what you're going to say. Let yourself be surprised by what you write.

When it comes to your plan for writing, hold the reins to your ideas loosely. If you write without having a firm control over where you're going, you may end up in some pretty cool places.

Listen with an attentive ear, an open heart, and a trusting mind. The more you do, the more words will come. And don't try too hard.

#4. Spelling, punctuation, grammar, and neatness do not matter in a first (or second) draft.

Perhaps you are a good speller, or maybe not. If you're writing in a notebook and you misspell a word, it doesn't matter.

The more I write, the worse my handwriting becomes. The point of this rule is to differentiate between the essence of your writing, its content, and the outward form. Address spelling, punctuation, and grammar after your initial drafts.

#5. There is no wrong way to write your poem: "Protect your vision."

Joni Mitchell says, "I believe a total unwillingness to cooperate is what is necessary to be an artist—not for perverse reasons, but to protect your vision." The artist is the one who sees another path, who wants to forge a path for herself (not necessarily for anyone else to follow) because the well-worn route doesn't go in the direction she wants go.

PART III

Who Said You Couldn't Say That?:
Twenty-Five Poetry-Writing
Suggestions in Twenty-One
Short Chapters

In the following pages are twenty-five invitations to your next poems. Take a look at which of these ideas strikes your interest, or choose a writing suggestion at random. Pick up your pen or your phone, your tablet or your laptop, and dive in, keeping in mind that there's no wrong way to write a poem. If you don't respond well to one idea, choose another. May you go forward with a fistful of pencils and a ream of poems.

35   *Writing Faster Than You Can Think*

Some years back, the poet Deena Metzger led a poetry workshop that I took part in. One of the writing exercises she taught us I've used and taught ever since: Writing Faster Than You Can Think.

It works well as a warm-up, as a way to circumvent the critic or conquer writer's block. It'll get you to surprising and unrestrained material, and lead you to your most authentic approach to writing poetry. Set the timer on your phone for one to three minutes.

Look around the room, notice what catches your attention, and write it down. Begin with single words or short phrases—"laughing girl," "sleeping boy," "gray bridge outside my window"—then move to entire sentences.

Quickly, you'll come up with surprising ways to describe what you see and how you feel about it, and find links between one seemingly unrelated thing and another: "The gray bridge across the water and all those driven stories, not far beyond my window stretched across the night."

Write as freely as you can—any and everything that comes to you. Include what's inside or outside the room, and that which is inside or outside your mind. If you get stuck as you're writing and no more words come, rewrite the last few words till something else arrives—it will. After time's up, stop and read what you've got.

Your writing may have left the room entirely, and you may find words before you that you've spent weeks looking for. They were hiding, waiting for a free and honest welcome in order to approach. Now you have material out of which to craft a poem; at the very least there may be a line or two that you would particularly like to pull out and develop.

If you've begun with two minutes, next time go for five, or as long as you want—as long as you're accepting of whatever words come.

36   I Remember: Memory and Poetry

Kathy, a student in one of my classes, wanted to write a poem about the day her brother died. He'd been young and his death had been unexpected. Kathy had tried to write about her loss several times, but she could barely remember anything about it. Though she knew there'd been a phone call informing her of his death, she couldn't remember the words that were spoken, nor who'd said them.

I suggested she begin by writing the words "I don't remember" and list the things she'd once known but, due to the impact of grief, had forgotten, such as "I don't remember what time of day the call came" and "I don't remember where I was." Not surprisingly, Kathy thought my idea was ridiculous—if you can't remember, you can't remember, right?

That evening, she emailed me. In the subject bar were the words "I remember!" By writing a list of all the things that she couldn't recall, accepting and not pushing against her lost memories, that which she thought was gone forever returned. Nothing is really lost to us. We remember a lot more than we may think we do, but sometimes memories go underground. Life is so full of experiences that we can't hold every story at the fore of our minds all the time. We may lose important memories—temporarily or permanently—because what happened is too painful to recall. Forgetting certain things may serve us when we are trying to move forward with our lives.

The other night, at a poetry reading for an anthology I co-edited, *Ink Knows No Borders: Poems of the Immigrant and Refugee Experience*, Marcelo Hernandez Castillo, the author of a collection of poetry titled *Cenzontle*, shared his work and talked about memory. He said that, because of trauma he endured growing up, there were years of his childhood that he couldn't remember at all. Slowly bits of memory are starting to return. He shares these with his wife, and later she retells him his life's stories. Through his wife's gifts of storytelling and love, Castillo's life is coming back to him, and he's beginning to recall more. Castillo told me, "I've been thinking of memory for a long time and what it means to have lost so much of it."

To write a poem about a particular time, you needn't remember any more than you do. Poems may be built from fragments, assorted threads that, through writing, are woven into new cloth. Keep in mind that the poem will not be a replica of what happened, even if you're writing about an event you recall in detail; it won't mirror what occurred. As we considered in this book's first section, there's the event itself and what you thought about it at the time, and there's what you think about it now. The emphasis of importance may shift. You may notice what went unnoticed when the event took place. Perhaps what was in the background or a side story will be what interests you now.

If you choose to write about something that's only a shadowy or partial memory, consider starting, like Kathy did, with the words "I don't remember." If remembering is the right thing, what you need to know will likely return.

37   Lost and Found

Anytime you lose one thing, something else is found. Lose your way, and chances are you'll notice the details of your surroundings as you wouldn't have otherwise: Was it here, at this power pole, that I turned right on the trail? Lose a person and you find an entire place within yourself that didn't exist before—that enormous hollow of absence.

In his poem "Maggie and milly and molly and may," E. E. Cummings said, "For whatever we lose(like a you or a me) / it's always ourselves we find in the sea." I've found that to be true. How about you?

When he was a little boy, poet Gary Young lost a sweater. Out playing one day, he put it down on a fence and when he went back to get it on his way home, it was gone. Young searched till nightfall but never found it, which led him to his first experience of doubt. "That was

the first time I had lost anything I really loved," he writes
in his poem "When I was five." "I knew my sweater
was not in heaven, but if it could disappear, just vanish
without reason, then I could disappear, and God might
lose me, no matter how good I was." Losing the sweater
caused him to remember it clearly. The poem concludes,
"The buttons on my sweater were translucent, a shimmer-
ing, pale opalescence. It was yellow." Have you ever lost
an object that was important to you, maybe when you
too were quite young? How'd you cope with that loss?
Was the item dropped or was it taken from you?

101

    When I was a young woman, some months after my
mother died, I had a garage sale to sell things of hers
neither my sister nor I had any use for. One small object
I let go of was a green cloisonné jar with a loose-fitting
lid. The moment the man put the money in my hand
and walked away with the jar, I wanted it back. Had I
needed yet another of my mother's tchotchkes? Not at
all. The lost jar made its way into a poem, and I remem-
ber it more clearly because, after letting it go, I found
it again in the poem. That lost item gained value not
because of itself but because, like my mother, it was
unreclaimable.

    Write about a time you lost something or somebody.
Start the poem in the present tense, as though it were
happening right now. That will return the experience to
you, giving it an immediacy that writing in the past tense
won't. But if that feels too close, try writing in the second
or third person and see where that takes you.

38 "I've Known Rivers"

In his poem "Year's End" Richard Wilbur wrote, "I've known the wind by water banks to shake / The late leaves down . . ." Such music in that! Langston Hughes wrote about knowing another part of the natural world in "The Negro Speaks of Rivers," written in 1920 when Hughes was seventeen, and when African Americans were commonly referred to as Negros. Recently out of high school, he was on a train heading from the Midwest of his childhood to Mexico City. When the train crossed the Mississippi, he wrote: "I've known rivers ancient as the world and older than the flow of human blood in human veins."

Notice the difference between "I've known," and "I know." "I know" is immediate, present tense, and authoritative, while "I've known" connotes the past and, to my ear, has a melancholy quality. One isn't better than the other, but with a change in form, a word's meaning can shift greatly.

What do you know? Earlier in the book we looked at our many ways of knowing. Now use an awareness of your multiple ways of knowing to lead you into writing a new poem. My guess is you know more than you realize. You know what's happened in your life, what you think, and how you feel—plenty of fuel for a poem. If you look back at your past, to your lived experiences, the stories you've heard and events you've read about, I'll bet you'll find material for a piece of writing.

Experiment with taking the same material and writing the poem two ways—beginning with "I've known" and "I

know." Notice how the same story will shift with just this
small change.

39   *These Are the Hands*

Gabriella Gutiérrez y Muhs, a poet I've known and loved
for decades, once gave me the coat off her back. It was
raining; she had a raincoat and I didn't. She draped
the stylish coat over my shoulders and refused to take
it back. A decade later, it's still my raincoat. Though
we shared an umbrella that morning, you know who
was the drier of the two. Another time, in preparation
for a reading we were giving, we went dress shopping.
Gabriella is one of those people who, like me, dresses
for the festival that life is and always wears lipstick. She
pulled a floor-length, velvet bodice dress off the rack
and instructed me to try it on though the cost was far
beyond my budget. Liking how it looked, she bought the
dress for me. Recently when she was in town we met for
coffee. In my rush to get to the café, I neglected to put
on earrings. "Patita," she said, "you're naked!" Reaching
into her bottomless purse, she pulled out the perfect
pair of earrings from Oaxaca and gave them to me.
Generosity is Gabita's backbone; it's her heartbeat.
    Gutiérrez y Muhs's parents were migrant workers who
followed the crops from Mexico to California. For over a
hundred years her family traveled back and forth across
the border that used to be a porous region. When the
family settled in Watsonville, her mother labored at the

cannery. Gutiérrez y Muhs knows what it means to do without and how to make something from nothing. She also knows what it is to be the first in her family to earn a PhD, a degree she received from Stanford University.

Ursula K. Le Guin said, "It is above all by the imagination that we achieve perception, compassion and hope." In her poem "These are the hands that could sand a wooden bench," Gabriella Gutiérrez y Muhs brings Le Guin's idea home to the page.

Here's her poem:

These are the hands that could sand a wooden bench

When I come by to deliver my burritos de papa con huevo,
they ask me, the men with silver caps on their teeth,
what church are you from?

Why did you come?
I bring burritos y café for you; I come from no church,
but my cousins are somewhere being fed by someone.
So, I thought I should come bring you my burritos de
*   huevo con papa,*
y salsa, something calientito to eat.

They smile their metal smiles as they hold my two babies,
and pass them around, kiss them and touch their nursed legs,
hold their hands and sit one of them on the back
of my station wagon, so they can share the baby,
like the Santo Niño de Atocha.
They stare at the other one, comment on his golden curls,
*   his soft skin.*

They laugh and encourage him as he farts,
on his production, encourage him to be human.
"Apriétele, mijo, con ganas."

They know a fat baby like the one their cousin has.
"Pura leche," they say, proud of my Mexican breasts,
and compliment my salsa, help me put things away, as a
    few of them leave.
The white men who collect them see me
and smirk. I must be someone's lover, they erroneously think,
stare at my huge milk breasts,
not understanding that breasts mean so much more than sex,
but I feel protected by the Mexican men, my new friends,
who would do anything for my sons and me, from now on,
because they know how to be graceful and grateful.
I know my father is watching with hope.

Theirs are the hands that never get lotion to put on their
    grietas,
from the construction work, the fields, the cleaning of
    people's garages,
the carrying buckets of God knows what, the shit they
    have to disappear,
the taking apart of debris they did not create, but must clean.

Theirs are the hands I shake when I arrive in limbo,
the hands that could sand a wooden bench,
the hands that become soft as they touch my babies
because they imagine their children in mine,
because they hold their children in deep embrace when
    they hold mine.

Consider writing about the place that empathy has in your own life—a time you offered compassion to another or a time it was freely given to you. Or write about sharing food with others as Gutiérrez does with the men outside Kmart who wait there each day in hopes of being hired to sand benches or dig ditches. You might

begin a poem with the words "These are the hands . . ." Or explore a time you felt a connection with a stranger or a group of strangers. A way to increase our happiness, recent research says, is to talk to someone you don't know. Could your poem be a father watching with hope, the arms that hold a baby, or a smile full of metal teeth? Might it have the piquancy of hot salsa or wrap up the essential as a tortilla does?

40 "A List of Further Possibilities"

Write a list poem as a way to riff on a subject. Begin by jotting down single words or short phrases on a particular topic. William Stafford wrote a poem called "What's in My Journal" that includes "Mean things, fishhooks, barbs in your hand. But marbles too."

To turn such a list into a poem, take it from being random to being considered. Notice how the poem changes when the order of the items on your list does. Each one makes way for the next—not in the first or second draft, but eventually, as you work with the material.

A list poem needs some details, but not all.

(Remember, a poet never gives everything away. That way there's room for readers to find themselves there.) Take a look at the opening of Chen Chen's "When I Grow Up I Want to Be a List of Further Possibilities," the title of which gives the reader an idea of what's coming:

To be a good   107
ex/current friend for R. To be one last

inspired way to get back at R. To be relationship advice for L. To be advice

for my mother. To be a more comfortable hospital bed for my mother. To be

no more hospital beds. To be, in my spare time, America for my uncle, who wants to be China

for me.

The poet Paola Capó-García likes writing list poems because, she says, "I'm interested in insistence." A list is a way to look at a single subject from multiple angles, and to both insist and persist.

41   *Who Said You Couldn't Say That?*

Is there something you want to write about that you've turned away from because you've been told it's not an acceptable subject for poetry, or because it's a story you think you should never reveal? Remember, if a subject repeatedly calls you over time, my experience—and the experience of many of my students and other poets—tells me you're ready to write it, to explore what you know to be true.

108   No poem that you write, especially if it's deeply personal, has to be shared. Much of what I write never gets beyond the notebook. Certain pieces get into final draft, but that still doesn't mean I'll let anyone else take a look. Some writing is meant only to be written, to take us to what's next. Poems are like stepping stones—each one leads to the writer's next poem.

If what you've written will hurt someone, as much as you needed to write it for yourself, detonating that bomb may not be the kind thing to do. Once I did just that. At a reading, I shared a poem in which I told a secret someone I loved had given me for safekeeping—and she was in the room at the time. (My stomach churns again just writing that.) It isn't something I'll ever do again, not without first clearing it with the person the poem is about.

Are there ten things, or two, that you believe you shouldn't say—from the not too important (your biology teacher's breath is the worst) to the terribly important (at this moment, you hate yourself)?

If you write the "forbidden" thing, watch what happens after the ink has soaked into the paper. At first you may feel a sense of embarrassment, as though you've written something you shouldn't have, or you may fear that there will be consequences. As long as you protect the work by keeping it private, that won't happen. (If that's not possible, destroying it may be the best option.) The feeling that comes next

is what will stay: a sense of liberty, of relief that arises from
an honest telling. To have said the thing you thought you
could never say. To see your brave words on the page.

42 *Your Very Human Body*

Where does breath come from? Ask Deema K. Shehabi.
In her poem "Breath," she writes, "You come to me from
the oldest wound of wind." Where does yours come
from? What great distance did the air have to travel to
become your inhalation?

Your body or someone else's may hold your next poem.
Consider your friend's hands at rest, the nape of your
own neck, the slope of waist moving down to the hip,
the arch of the foot, the turned back, your sweetheart
with her eyes closed. Or laughter, the loping run, hands
kneading bread dough, the sound of your mother weep-
ing. Choose an aspect of this body and write what you
know, what you see, what you desire.

43 *The Love Poem*

What would a book about writing poetry be without
discussion of the love poem? Heartless, that's what.
Here's a challenge: write a love poem without using
the word "love." Not once, not anywhere. "Love" is a
problematic word when it comes to poetry because it's

been overused to the point of having become vacuous. The word "heart" too: stay clear of that one. When a word gets over used, it becomes cliché, which makes it incapable of conjuring the emotion that it was intended to.

The best poems give us the *why* of the matter through the telling of the *what*. Make your reader see what you see and love who you love by describing what happened.

You might start with a very small action—how they stand so close you breathe their breath. Jason, a student of mine, wrote, "It's the way she turns that I like." Even though the girl was leaving him, he was enamored of her moves.

In her poem ,"The Sword Swallower's Valentine," Sandra Beasley has this line: "Your smile is the strike of a match." Need she say more? What would you give for that smile?

Sonia Sanchez was a haiku master. Here's one, "Blues Haiku":

> *let me be yo wil*
> *derness let me be yo*
> *wind blowing you all day.*

Three lines and there you have it. Instead of the word "passion," Sanchez has the real thing.

> *You meet someone and inside of them*
> *you know there swells*
> *a small country brimming*
> *with steel and beasts of labor.*

So writes David Welch in "You Meet Someone and

Later You Meet Their Dancing and You Have to Start Again." Feel the seduction of that attraction.

Have you ever been in love, or "in like"? What qualities drew you to that person? Or if you're in love now, what qualities keep you in that altered, barely breathing state? Maybe make a list of them. Or choose a single thing that has your attention, and start your poem with that. Remember: not the word "love," or a Valentine "heart," anywhere.

44 Twenty Questions That Ask but Do Not Answer

Initially, it was said that the Nobel Prize–winning Chilean poet Pablo Neruda's death in 1973 was caused by cancer. Many were doubtful because he hadn't been that ill. Some believed it was grief that killed him. Two weeks before Neruda died, his country had been taken over by a US-backed coup d'état. While Neruda lay on his sickbed, soldiers assassinated the democratically elected president Salvador Allende, a close friend of the poet. Recently Neruda's remains were exhumed and scientists determined cancer was not the cause of death. Rather, it appears that the poet was poisoned—most likely because of his political work and his alliance with Allende's government.

Following Neruda's death, several completed poetry manuscripts were found on his desk. Among these volumes was *El libro de las preguntas* (*The Book of Questions*). The entire volume poses questions—over 300 in 74 poems—without a single answer. And isn't that how life feels some days? Neruda's are a particular kind of question: those that are unanswerable. The questions strike the reader with wonder.

Take Neruda's lead and write a poem consisting of a collection of your own unanswerable questions. Or write your questions down, choose one, and using your wildest imagination, answer it. Let yourself be playful, extravagant, absurd!

Here are a few of Neruda's questions to lead you to your own:

> *Do leaves secretly live*
> *in the roots in winter?*

> *What did the tree learn of the earth*
> *to confide to the sky?*
> *(from poem XLI)*

> *If all the rivers are sweet*
> *where does the sea get its salt?*
> *(from poem LXXII)*

45 Did I Hear That Right?: Overheard Conversations Transformed into Poems

Perhaps your mother has noticed, as mine did, your tendency to lean into other people's conversations, and perhaps she has told you that it's rude to eavesdrop. You could tell her that, as a poet, listening in on others is your job. Because it is. The writer needs to be attentive to whatever grabs his attention.

An overheard conversation could be the bones of a piece you write or the material may require you to add nothing more, as in "The Twenty-Third of January" by Amanda Torroni, from her book *Poetic Conversations*, which grew out of her Instagram series. In the introduction to the book, she says, "There is poetry in the way we speak to one another. In our exchanges. In the silence between phrases."

> *"I've never gotten a tattoo. What does it feel like?"*
> *"It feels like any other kind of art. It hurts a little."*

My father was quite skilled at finding money and other valuables that others had dropped. When an object on the sidewalk caught his eye, he'd bend down but look in another direction, so that if a passerby were to notice him, she would turn to see what my dad was looking at rather than the cash he was about to pick up. The same goes for listening to others. The best place for listening in on a conversation is somewhere crowded, where there are multiple conversations going on at the same time—buses and subway cars, a bustling café—and where you'll go unnoticed. To become a more refined eavesdropper, stand close to a conversation, but not so close that the parties cease their chat.

As long as you're not using overheard material to hurt someone and you keep their identity out of the poem, there's nothing wrong with building a piece of writing around an overheard conversation. It's a great way to extend your thinking beyond where it might naturally go.

A group of people in England formed what they

called the Bug Initiative, inviting writers across the
UK to eavesdrop on conversations over a single day to
create a new piece of writing. Their book *Bugged . . .
Writings from Overhearings* was the result. Consider a
conversation-gathering day with poet friends to scout
for your next poems. Later come together to share what
you heard and how you transformed conversations into
poems.

My friend Cheryl says that when she gets challenged
for staring, she responds, "Sorry, I was just spacing out
and daydreaming." Maybe that'll work for you too.

46   *The Found Poem*

Raymond Carver, best known for his short stories, was
also a poet. His last poetry collection, *A New Path to the
Waterfall*, included found poems that he created from
fragments of Anton Chekhov's short stories. He pulled
a brief passage from a story, and without changing any
of Chekhov's words, without rearranging them, and
without adding any of his own text, just by breaking
the excerpt into lines, Carver "found" the poem and
then gave it his own title. Carver's found poems draw a
reader's attention to small portions of Chekhov's stories
so that we notice the fragment more closely than we'd be
likely to when reading the stories as a whole.

Here's the conclusion to Carver's "Night Dampness."
(Note that a "sterlet" is a kind of fish.)

> *He tells me that this dark, forbidding river*
> *abounds in sterlet, white salmon, eel-pout, pike, but*
> *there is no one*
> *to catch the fish, and no tackle to catch it with.*

Material can be found wherever the written word is—
emails, texts, books, magazines, advertisements, billboards.
Copy lines from a newspaper or magazine article, rearrange
them, add some words of your own. Or find a discarded
book and, with marker or paint, cover over the parts of the
text you wish to remove from your poem. You could also
choose a theme and find passages from several sources on
that theme and build your poems from those. (Keeping in
mind that, in order to not plagiarize, anytime we borrow the
words of another writer we need to credit that writer.)

By incorporating text that's not our own into our
writing, we can expand our thinking. It's liberating, and
useful, especially on days when you're feeling distanced
from your creative self.

47   A Walk in the Dark

Take a nighttime walk alone, if that's safe (or with
another, if that's smarter); ideally, it should be a silent
walk. If you're walking in a barely lit place, carry a
flashlight to use if necessary, but if you can, let your
eyes adjust to the reduction of light so that you can see
what may be hidden. If you can't get outside, stare out
a nighttime window for a while. Or sit in a darkened

room and notice how the objects slowly emerge from that darkness and appear differently than they do in the light.

There are layers and variations of darkness—the true blacks, the dark blues, and the pale grays. If you are out walking, note how movement appears differently without much light, and how it feels to strain to see. Your other senses will do double duty to compensate for what your eyes can't tell you. Does the lack of light cause you to hear more?

Is there an aspect of night that you like best—stars, moon, or the limited amount of light? In his poem "Brotherhood," Mexican poet, Octavio Paz, winner of the Nobel Prize in Literature in 1990, wrote:

> *I look up:*
> *the stars write.*
> *Unknowing I understand:*
> *I too am written,*
> *and at this very moment*
> *someone spells me out.*

Perhaps you too are written there.

When you get to a lighted place, pull out your notebook or your phone and find the poem in what you've seen and imagined.

48 "I Had Too Much to Dream Last Night"

Some mornings, you wake up more exhausted than the moment your head hit the pillow the night before. Your body may have been nicely tucked in between the sheets for several hours; but your mind, that's another story. You had too much to dream, that's all. That's how the '60s rock band The Electric Prunes referred to one of those dream-tormented nights.

Dream-drenched, you might find yourself in poetry paradise. Images and stories that come from our dreams are often crazy and surreal: a lion stands on his hind legs and knocks at your front door, or you scream so loudly skyscrapers fall and cars skid along the street. These quirky images are perfect material for poetry. The absurdity of them surprises, and that's one thing a poem ought to do.

Antonio Machado, the Spanish poet, wrote:

> *Last night as I was sleeping,*
> *I dreamt—marvelous error!—*
> *that I had a beehive*
> *here inside my heart.*

Like Machado, you could begin a poem with the words "Last night" and follow them with what you dreamt. Choose the essence, the dream's strongest images.

Or leave the dream itself behind. Toni, a writing student of mine, shared this:

> *Day dreaming,*
> *night dreaming, whatever.*
> *It's the only second language I know.*

Not until Toni wrote that did I consider dreaming

to be a language, but now I'm all in. Perhaps it's the language of night, which lets us write most freely about our deepest or craziest desires.

49   Fear and What Eases It a Little

In his poem, "Middle Passage," Robert Hayden wrote:

> *I cannot sleep, for I am sick*
> *with fear, but writing eases fear a little*

Who, at times, like Hayden, hasn't been "sick with fear"—when your heart threatens to pound right out of your chest and the breath comes shallow? There's a lot about life that can be frightening. Even the tree's shadow at the window can look like a human until you know for sure that it's not.

How do you respond to fear? You might follow Hayden and talk back to what frightens you in a poem. I've found writing to be my best way to counter it. In a letter, Emily Dickinson wrote, "And so I sing, as the boy does by the burying ground, because I am afraid." Writing is another kind of song. Next time you're scared, reach for paper and pencil.

Maya Angelou opens her poem "Life Doesn't Frighten Me" this way:

> *Shadows on the wall*
> *Noises down the hall*
> *Life doesn't frighten me at all.*

She's trying to convince herself that she's not afraid.
Once fear is down on paper, you can get distance from it
and see it as distinct from the whole of who you are, and
that decreases its dimensions.

Either look back at something that frightened you in
the past or look at what's frightening you lately. Watch
that fear shrink once you capture it in a poem.

50 My Birth and My Name: "at the rupture where land became ocean"

Here's Safia Elhillo's poem "Yasmeen" in its entirety:

i was born	*i was planted*
at the rupture the root where	*land became ocean became land anew*
split from my parallel self i split from	*its shape refusing root in my fallow mouth*
the girl i also could have been	*cleaving my life neatly*
& her name / easy / i know the story	*& my name / taken from a dead woman*
all her life / my mother wanted	*to remember / to fill an aperture with*
a girl named for a flower	*cut jasmine in a bowl*
whose oil scents all	*our longing*
our mothers /	*our mothers'*
petals wrung	*wilting*
for their perfume	*garlands hanging from our necks*

Elhillo's poem is verb-lush. It splits, cleaves, cuts,
refuses. The more you use verbs to describe, as opposed
to relying on adjectives, the stronger your work will
be. The verb allows a reader to move with you. Verbs

are words of change, and that's more dynamic that a stationary adjective.

"Yasmeen" is lush not only in verbs but in meaning. And form, oh, what she does with form! Notice that this skillful poem can be read in more ways than one. You can read each column of the poem individually and you can also read it all the way across, inclusive of both columns.

Consider writing two poems in one—a two-columned poem. Experiment with empty space, and notice how the break between two columns influences meaning. Do you end up with two poems? A conversation poem could be written this way: one person speaks in one column and the other in the second one.

Here are some other ideas for poems that I find in "Yasmeen" (you'll likely find more):

Start out as she has with "I was born . . ." Where were you born? Name the place or give it to us through description alone. Or begin with "I was planted . . ." "Planted" is, of course, typically what's done with a seed. Are we not like seeds too in some ways, able to thrive more vigorously in certain soil than in others?

Were you born in one location and later planted in another? Do you carry two or more places within yourself? To which do you belong—either, both, or neither? And if you moved often as a child, does movement itself become a way of life? A friend of mine grew up in a military family and then married a military man; she has moved thirty times over the course of her life—so far.

All the verbs in this poem—"born," "split," "planted," "refusing," "cleaving"—make me wonder: Which are your truest moves? Begin by making a list of the verbs that describe you best—go crazy with it. Do you swim, fall, crave, step, run? Or sizzle, fry, squeeze, engulf? Even the smallest actions count: "I mull"; "I breathe"; "I wait." Be expansive; lie. Where does moving take you? Add the place where you do these things: in a sheltered neighborhood, in a smothering desert? Build this poem one movement at a time.

Then there's the opposite—verb-less poems. In Ed Hirsh's book *A Poet's Glossary*, he writes, "The verbless poem can create a static quality, a sense of the arrested movement." He references a fourteen-word poem by Ezra Pound, "In a Station of the Metro," that hasn't a single verb. (It is interesting also for the way its words move across the page):

> *The apparition of these faces in the crowd;*
> *Petals on a wet, black bough.*

Though not a strict haiku, Pound based his poem on that form, with its aspects of nature and surprise. Even without a verb, I imagine movement here—the faces looking around and the rain wetting the petals.

51   "Nothing's Left"

> *Nothing's left to say between us*
> *everything went into the train that hid its whistle*
> *in the smoke that didn't become a cloud*
> *in the departure that gathered your limbs . . .*

That's from "Handkerchief," by Palestinian poet Ghassan Zaqtan. Have you had times when you too felt there was nothing left to say, even to a best-beloved, when a relationship had gone as far as it could, and that was it?

Take yourself back in memory to a moment of futility or finality; or think about the experience of someone you know; or imagine your way into this poem. Begin with the words Zaqtan used: "Nothing's left."

Or take this approach: in her poem "Day by Day," one of my students, Saroj Groebler, wrote a poem about moving away.

> *Day by day*
> *they come.*
> *They come and*
> *take everything.*
> *Everything*
> *but a small feather.*
> *A feather that makes*
> *everything wonderful*
> *again.*
> *I*
> *will*
> *use*
> *it*
> *soon.*

If nearly nothing's left, does one thing remain? Might something ordinary gain extraordinary power at a desperate time, like Saroj's feather? (And note that her poem is a shape poem—there's that feather!)

52   The Lost Words

In the beautifully illustrated book *The Lost Words*, author
Robert Macfarlane and illustrator Jackie Morris created
a tribute to the words our world is losing. Yup, words are
leaving our language. Why? Because they aren't being   123
used.

In his introduction, Macfarlane writes, "The words . . .
disappeared so quietly that at first almost no one
noticed." Throughout the book, the disappearing words
are hidden and peeking through illustrations of grass,
leaves, seaweed. For a very long time, these words for
parts of nature—"acorn," "bluebell," "bramble," "king-
fisher"—were commonplace.

Now that most of us dwell in urban areas, we've lost
much of our connection to the earth. Not only are words
such as "wren" being lost, but due to global warming,
the places where many creatures live are endangered.
According to the United Nations, a million species are at
risk of extinction as the result of human activities.

In China, there are no longer many bees. That means
that humans have to do the job that bees have always done
for free, for their own sustenance. People climb ladders
and brush some manmade pollinating concoction on the
flowering trees. (You can see photos of this process online.)
Meanwhile, in Africa, giraffes are nearing extinction. Did
you know that the last male white rhino has died?

Ah, but the great California condor is returning, and
over the past three decades, the population of grizzly
bears in the Greater Yellowstone Ecosystem has been

growing. The use of the pesticide DDT nearly eradicated the bald eagle from New Jersey, but as of 2015, there were 161 pairs, up from only one pair in the 1970s. And though these declines were the result of human behavior, people are also behind the protection and breeding of these nearly lost animals.

124   For this poem, choose an animal or a plant that's endangered and learn what you can about it. Take bits of that information along with your own thoughts and feelings and blend them to form a poem for that being. Or consider the idea of endangered species and extinction in other ways. Is there something about you or someone you love that's endangered? Do you have a dream that you fear is about to go extinct?

53   *Into the Future: Take Yourself There Now*

Is the future a place you wish you could arrive at now? I remember feeling that way.

Or maybe here and now is fine. For the length of a poem, venture into that place called future, as you imagine it; peer into its unknown terrain, and see what you find. My student Rachel B. wrote:

> *The future is as blurry*
> *as when you splash water*
> *and try to see your reflection*

And another student, Karen Amundson, wrote:

> *Future is inside me,*
> *right beyond this storm of hope.*

How do you see your future? Is it also just beyond a
storm of hope?   125

54   A Formal Form for Fun (and Hopefully Not Too Much Frustration):

THE GHAZAL

Ghazals are poems about love, loss, or longing, but
they aren't narratives. This Arabic word is pronounced
"guzzle." Written in a minimum of five couplet stanzas
and typically no more than fifteen, the last word or
phrase of each couplet remains the same throughout the
entire poem, and the second-to-last word of each couplet
rhymes. Often, the poet's own name appears somewhere
in the poem. In the poem's first couplet the same phrase
concludes both lines. Each of the poem's lines should be
the same length.

The poet Agha Shahid Ali popularized this form
among American poets. Here are two stanzas from his
poem simply titled "Ghazal."

> *I'll do what I must if I'm bold in real time.*
> *A refugee, I'll be paroled in real time.*

Cool evidence clawed off like shirts of hell-fire?
A former existence untold in real time . . .

A recent ghazal, "That's My Heart Right There"
by Willie Perdomo (yes, he uses the word "heart" in
his poem—for every rule, an exception), takes a bit of
freedom with the form. Here it is in its entirety:

We used to say,
That's my heart right there.

As if to say,
Don't mess with her right there.

As if, don't even play,
That's a part of me right there.

In other words, okay okay,
That's the start of me right there.

As if, come that day,
That's the end of me right there.

As if, push come to shove,
I would fend for her right there.

As if, come what may,
I would lie for her right there.

As if, come love to pay,
I would die for that right there.

55   Five for Five

Here are five writing prompts that require no more than five minutes to get a draft started. Remember, there's great advantage to speed in the initial writing process. You might consider them warm-ups to lubricate the imagination muscle.

* Look out a window. Write what you see. Now stand outside that window. What do you see looking in?

* Complete the following sentence and see where you end up: "My mother's eyes . . ." What do you think they see? What do you see when you look at her? Change out the person: "My friend's eyes . . . ," "My grandfather's eyes . . ."

Marjorie Agosín begins her poem "My Mother's Eyes":

> *My mother's eyes*
>
> *are cities*
> *where birds*
> *nest*
> *where voyages of the ill-fated*
> *come to rest*
> *where water is a mirror*
> *of sung secrets.*

* At the moment, what's your favorite word? Do you like it for its meaning or its sound? Write an acrostic poem using that word. Write the word vertically and begin a phrase with that letter. Each line can be a whole sentence, or you can write a single-sentence poem this way. Your poem may be long and complex, or short and simple like mine. California's drought is being alleviated a bit by today's rain, making that my favorite word:

> *Ragged*
> *Attention, mine,*
> *Is taken by that*
> *Not noise outside the window but longed for rain.*

* Take an emotion. Say, happiness. If you could see happiness, what would you see? And what if you could smell, taste, feel, and hear it? Write those words or phrases down. You can take the descriptions you come up with and use them as the basis of your next poem.

* Trace the outline of your hand on a piece of paper. That perimeter is the line for your poems. Write about the places your hand has taken you, what it's touched and held, the softest things, the roughest, the lightest, and the heaviest. Or fill the interior space of your hand using experiences of touch as the poem's foundation.

PART IV

"How Possible Might
the Impossible Be?":
Getting Your Poems
Out There

Now that you've been writing for a while, now that poems are at least sometimes easy under your pen, we'll look at some of the more practical aspects of writing poetry, getting your poems into the world and living the poet's life.

56   Success and Failure

At first, success is in the writing of poems. Questions like "Is this a good poem?" come later. That way, you learn with freedom and curiosity how to do a new thing.

After a while, I'll bet you will begin to want to know which of your poems are strongest and come closest to being whole and authentic, free from the need to explain a thing. At that point, you'll be ready to bring them into the world, in whatever ways suit you best.

In the next chapter, on editing and revision, we'll dive into what makes a poem work. But for now, let's think about the idea of success and failure. Look at "the making of poems" by Lucille Clifton.

> *the reason why i do it*
> *though i fail and fail*
> *in the giving of true names*
> *is i am adam and his mother*
> *and these failures are my job.*

To view failure as what a poet is supposed to do—to consider it part of one's job—is counterintuitive. We tend to think not only that failure is a hindrance to success, but that it's bad—or worse, that we are bad when we don't succeed. Of course, success is what we strive for, and to get there, we should avoid failure at all costs, right?

Ever since I heard Clifton read this poem, her voice, particularly when she got to the pronouncement at the end—"these failures are my job"—has lived in me and offered comfort. It helps me to be more accepting of the truth of the writing experience. To become a strong writer, you have to try things out and to dare.

There will be many false starts, a lack of clarity and precision in your language, unintentional redundancies, poems that start off strong but fizzle out. You'll write poems that will stall or fall flat on their pretty poetic faces. Then comes the subsequent deleting or ripping to shreds, or fireplace burning, of work that dead-ends, that sadly goes nowhere.

But wait: all of your poems are going somewhere! Keep in mind, every poem you write increases your skill; each poem helps you hone your vision, develop your style, refine your chosen subject matter, take creative leaps, and learn to trust your imagination.

When I get frustrated with writing—at being unable to say the thing I want to say—my husband will remind me, "You're not digging a ditch, you know." If you have a shovel and a plot of dirt that needs digging, and your body is strong, it's straightforward hard work. By day's end, you'll be tired and may have blisters, but, hopefully, some money and a cold drink too (and a nice deep ditch!). Creativity can be fickle. It can be complicated. It's easy to lose a train of thought, to write yourself into a corner.

To invest in your writing, you have to give it the time it needs when it's easy and when it's hard. Here's a story about Lucille Clifton. She came to Santa Cruz to give a reading when she was elderly and not physically strong. Before the crowd, the content of her work was as strong as ever, but her voice, though beautiful, had lost some of its force.

Partway through the reading, a man in the audience yelled out, "Speak louder, please." Even from the back of the room, I could see the fire in Clifton's eyes. Leaning forward, she said, "Listen harder!" Oh, such beautiful fury!

I tell you this story now because it's the attitude that will support your writing through your successes and failures. When you get frustrated because your writing is off the mark, and you want to say to yourself, "Write better," instead do what Clifton did: stand firm and determined, confident. You will find your way.

57   Making Your Words Stick to the Page: The Editing Process

After writing a poem, I put it in an actual or an imaginary drawer for a while. I want the words to get to know each other in the arrangement I've given them. Will they become allies? Or are they going to tear each other up, so that when I go back for the poem I'll find only paper shards?

Getting some space from the poem allows me to see it

more clearly, as separate from myself. Turning back to it, I become not only its writer but its first reader.

Here's what I look for: Does the poem make something happen in my body? Does it startle or cause tears to come to the edges of my eyes? Make me angry, poem! Make me fall in love. A poem that causes me to think anew, or that reminds me of something important I'd forgotten, is the poem I want to read. Look at a handful of favorite poems that others have written. What draws you in and holds your attention? Is it the unexpected subject matter? The imagery the poet uses? Make a list of the qualities that get to you.

Next, look at your own work. Does it have the same qualities? What does your work need to do to be moving or subtle or edgy, or whatever you're after?

When it comes to editing, I always read the poem aloud. When I do that, at some point along the way, a buzzer in my head may go off. So, I reread the line that caused that awful noise. If it goes off again, that indicates something in the line is off. That buzzer is spot-on in informing me of when I'm being disingenuous or unclear. It informs me the poem needs more work.

I may read it to a trusted someone. Because it's not their poem, they may be able to see it more clearly than I can and tell me what's not working. I have notebooks of lines that I've reluctantly deleted from poems, to keep for a rainy day.

My goal, before I call a poem complete (knowing that a poem is a malleable thing that I may want to revise again later), is to be able to say "yes" to every single word and its relationship to every other word. This line, attributed to William Stafford, describes what we might all strive for in our poems: "If one part were touched, the whole would tremble." Have you ever touched a spider's delicate web and noticed how that's exactly what happens?

That trembling comes because there's a relationship between all the parts of a finished poem. A strong poem equals more than the sum of its components. For the writer, and later the reader, to be moved by a poem, the language needs to resonate emotionally. For this to happen, a kind of magic needs to occur that allows writing to go beyond the intellect. I see it as welcoming the spirit in. Be sure, when editing your writing, that you don't edit the magic out.

Years ago, I wrote a poem while staying in a cabin alone, in Desolation Wilderness, California—no phone, no electricity, no car, only a rowboat (that I couldn't adequately row) to get around Echo Lake. Each day, I hiked for miles into the granite, and each day, I wrote. One day, this line came to me: "It is so quiet my mother could be alive." Wait a minute—no matter how quiet a day may be, dead is dead; not even the greatest silence can bring her back. But that line resonated, and though I can't apply logic to it, it works.

Part of poetry's magic comes from its open spaces. The reader can enter into what's not on the page but is implied. If too much is said, if a poem is full of particular details that pertain only to the poet, then the reader is left out. If a poem is too vague, too general, then the reader can't find the door to get inside.

During the editing process choose what to keep and

what to let go of. The *how* of doing this develops over time. In addition to reading your new poem a few times and then putting it away for a bit, here are some pointers for editing your poems:

* Have you created an experience, a picture, or a story, for your reader?

* How does it sound? Read the poem aloud, listening not only for the authenticity of the content but for how it sounds. Do the word sounds support the meaning?

* Are all the words essential? In my draft poems I often say something, and then say it again in another way to be sure I've really conveyed it. Once is enough! If you're clear, your reader will get it.

* Check your punctuation. Do each of the punctuation marks support the poem's meaning and sound?

* How does it look on the page? Type your poem up at least three different ways by changing where you break the lines until you come to what resonates best with what you're saying in this poem. Does the poem have stanzas? If so, remember, the stanza is to poetry what the paragraph is to prose.

58 *Not by Any Other Name: Titling Your Poems*

In his almost-acceptance note, the editor of a literary journal wrote to say that because I'd used the poem's last line as its title, it was as though I'd given the punch line away before I told the joke. They would like to publish the poem in their magazine, he wrote, *if* I gave it a new title. The editor was right, but I was flummoxed, and there was a firm deadline. The poem had been inspired by the Fellini film *La Dolce Vita*. After some thought, I changed "Like Birds Taking Flight in the Italian Sky" to "*Sotto, Sotto*," Italian words meaning "softly, softly."

A poem's title may be what gets someone to read the poem. When I pick up a collection of poetry, I'll leaf through the book till I come to a compelling title. The poem's title should tell a little about it, but as the magazine editor pointed out to me, it should neither give the ending away nor tell too much about what the reader will find within. A title is a little tease. It needs to add something to the poem, not duplicate what's already there.

Some poets take the first line of their poem and also use it as the title. This can give the first line the incantatory force of repetition and is a time-honored technique. Mostly, I choose words that aren't already in the poem. Occasionally, I'll find words from the body of the poem that I think warrant more notice and use those for the title.

When you're ready to title your poem, try a few on for size till you land on the word or words that, once on the page, feel like they've always been there.

59 *Time for a Trustworthy Reader?*

As a writer, you need to know that what you *think* is on the page is actually there and not only in your head. A reader whose opinion you can trust is invaluable.

Since just after high school, my best friend Gina has been my go-to person. She's not a poet and she doesn't read much poetry, but she is smart, has a big heart, and knows how to listen. She may not offer technical help but when she says, "Something is off right here," she's usually right.

As in much of life, it's important to ask for what you want. After you've chosen a reader, consider what kind of feedback you want. "Please tell me what you like about this poem" is a great place to start. If your reader can't or won't tell you what they like, they're not the right reader. The person you choose needs to respect you and be willing to take direction.

Be as specific as you can when asking for feedback: "Does this line hold up? What does it tell you?" Asking questions of your reader will let them know what you're after.

You might want to know:

* Do you get confused anywhere?

* Is my poem easy or difficult to follow?

* Anything missing?

* Does it move you?

* Is it believable? Do I sound authentic?

* How do you feel after having read it?

* I'm stuck on this part of the poem. Would you help me
figure out why?

   Some poems, no matter how hard we work on them,
are never going to be finished. There's a poem that I
began writing on a Greek island many years ago about
an elderly man and his mule. I love parts of it—but as a
whole the poem doesn't work, no matter that I've tried
for a long time to get it right. Every now and again, I
pull it out, tinker a bit, and then, frustrated, put it away.
Maybe someday. Remember what we talked about
earlier: writing one poem will lead you to the next one,
even if that poem is a failed attempt. You need your
failures as much as or more than you *need* your successes.
That's the way we learn. I'll bet you're progressing
beautifully along your path.

60   *Open Your Notebook and
         Let Your Poems Out*

After you've been writing for a while, and are beginning
to feel a sense of your identity as a poet, and your
confidence is growing, you'll likely want to take your

poems to another level. Consider participating in open mics or slams at coffee shops. You might join—or start—a school poetry club. Maybe you want to begin sending your work out to be considered for publication? There are lots of online and print literary journals that welcome the work of new writers.

140   Poet Sara Michas-Martin says, "Try to think about publishing only after you feel true ownership of the work. When I feel I have two or three poems that make a nice group I send them out to journals that I read and admire . . . This means I read a lot of journals. I also take note of where the poets I admire publish their work and I read those journals (libraries are often the best place to discover journals devoted to publishing poetry) . . . I don't send anything out until I'm confident the poem is fully realized and what I want to say has made it onto the page. This can take a very long time. Sometimes years."

Before you jump into sending your work out, consider this point, also from Sara Michas-Martin: "The desire to publish can be poison to creative process. If you write only to be published you are giving someone else the power to validate your voice and attempt at creative expression. That's not to say that putting your work out there is not important. Your voice matters, your voice should be heard."

When you are ready, research journals to see which ones publish poems that resonate with what you're writing. If you search for "literary journals" online, a raft of sites will come up. Be sure to check them out before sending them your poems. It can be expensive to purchase an issue from several journals. Instead, go to your local bookstore or library or ask your school's English department, and ask other poets what journals they like and if you could borrow a copy.

When it comes to deciding where to send your poems, not only do you need to determine whether the site or publication is a good fit, but you also need to figure out if it is legit. There are many sites calling themselves "poetry contests," and sure, they are, but they charge $25 or so to look at your poems. For better or worse, that's a very standard reading fee for contests. I know poets who've spent a few hundred dollars and gotten published and others who spent similar amounts and didn't have any luck. Look closely before sending your work.

Some contests don't ask for any money upfront. Instead they send you a letter of congratulations, informing you that you are one of the winners and a note that "For only $50, you'll get your poem published." Those who fall for this do get published and months later in the mail what they receive is reminiscent of a dictionary—a hardback tome that's stuffed with two columns' worth of poems printed on onion-skin paper. If you read through it, you'll see that the work wasn't vetted; they publish whatever comes to them, by whoever will pay the fee to see their poem in print. Be cautious of any competition offering $10,000 in prize money! Here are a few to stay clear of: America Library of Poetry, International Poetry Digest, The National Amateur Poetry Competition, and Poetry Unlimited. (If you're unsure, take a look at this site: https://winningwriters. com/the-best-free-literary-contests/contests-to-avoid/.)

To figure out which journals are legit and which are

bogus, look at the names associated with the publication. Are these people whose poetry books you've read? If it looks fishy, chances are it is. Ask another poet or a teacher what they think. Google the name of the publication and see what comes up.

Before sending your poems out into the world to honest publishers, it's important to be sure that your poems are ready, and that you are. When you begin to make your work public, either through a poetry performance of one kind or another or by sending poems to magazines, your skin ought to have some thickness to it.

If you send a packet of poems out and you get critiqued by an editor, remember that person is critiquing your poems, not you. Because you're the writer, you're going to be close to the poetry you write, and closer to some poems than others. A poem, no matter how much you love it, is something of your creation; it is not you. Repeat after me: "My poem isn't me!" It'll help if you can develop an attitude of hoping for acceptance but remaining prepared for rejection.

Online submission platforms like Submittable (https://www.submittable.com) and Teen Ink (https://www.teenink.com/) make sending your poems out very easy.

My suggestion is to get organized. Keep a chart of where you've sent your work and where you'll try next.

61 Sound Check: Reading and Performing Your Poems

A poem can silently sing and shout from the page, but when it's read aloud it can do much more. Your voice is an instrument—you can adjust its tone, volume and force and, in that way, bring your poems to life.

Listen and watch other poets giving voice to their work, so that you can take in the possibilities that exist in the dance between voice and breath and sound and body movement and facial expression and silence. How quiet can you make your voice? When your voice is loud, can it remain nuanced?

In addition to going to slams and readings, here are some resources for listening to poetry online:

* At the Library of Congress's Archive of Recorded Poetry and Literature site, you can listen to poets long gone from the world read their poetry, such as Elizabeth Bishop, Robert Frost, and Audre Lorde. You can also hear recordings by many contemporary poets, such as Sandra Cisneros, Alberto Ríos, and Tracy K. Smith (who's got a terrific podcast, called The Slowdown, in which she reads poems by other writers). (https://www.loc.gov/collections/archive-of-recorded-poetry-and-literature/about-this-collection/)

* Poets.org has many recordings, including poems by Camille T. Dungy, Yusef Komunyakaa, Rachel Eliza

Griffiths, and Richard Blanco. (https://www.poets.org/
poetsorg/poems)

* On Poetry Out Loud's website you'll hear such actors
as Angela Lansbury and Anthony Hopkins performing
poems. Poet Kay Ryan reads Leigh Hunt's "Jenny Kiss'd
Me," and Paul Laurence Dunbar's "We Wear the Mask"
is read by Rita Dove. (https://www.poetryoutloud.org/
poems-and-performance/listen-to-poetry)

Begin by reading other people's poems aloud. Read
the same poem several times and alter your approach
to it—experimenting with volume, pitch, timbre, and
timing. Choosing another's poem will be less personal
than reading your own, and you'll be able to get a more
objective sense of what reading style best supports the
poem's content. Then move on to doing this with your
own poems. Try standing in front of the mirror and
reading to yourself.

When we read in front of others, many of us tend to
clam up; nervousness constricts the voice. Nothing is
better for this than breathing deeply—bring the air in
with ease, not force. Thinking of your voice as coming
from your belly, or, better yet, all the way up from the
earth, lends the necessary strength.

Taylor Mali, who has won many national slam con-
tests, says that biting into an apple before reciting helps
him because it creates saliva, and adds that he doesn't
drink too much water so he won't have to take a bath-
room break!

Before giving a reading, consider that you're nervous

because you're getting ready to do something important. Nerves aren't bad if they propel us forward, but they're a hindrance when they hold us back.

After you've got a few poems that you feel comfortable with, take them into the world. Will you read them from the page or memorize them? Either way, allow yourself to fully inhabit the poems and to engage with your audience—look either at their faces or right above their heads. They won't know you're not looking at them, but they'll feel welcomed into your work.

62   *Alternatives to Traditional Publishing*

In your infinite creativity, you may want to do something entirely different from the traditional approach. Many poets are coming up with inventive ways to get their poems into the world. Here are some possibilities:

* Start a blog: Perhaps a blog on given themes where fellow poets can share their work too.

* Post poems on Twitter: A new genre of poetry exists because of Twitter's short form.

* Make a broadside: Usually a broadside, or poetry poster, features a single poem, illustrated or not. It can be printed on heavy paper, right from your computer or at a copy shop. Some of my favorites are no bigger than a postcard. A letterpress broadside is a beautiful (and

not inexpensive) thing; perhaps there's such a printer not far from you. Or check out Etsy's custom letterpress printing options. Poem broadsides make great gifts. You can post them on the walls of your school (if they'll let you) or at a local café, or sell them at poetry events.

146

* Make your own chapbook: You don't need a publisher for this. There are computer programs that you can use to create books, or you can go to your local copy shop and tell them what you'd like to do. I often make these and give them as gifts. Sometimes I make an illustration for the front.

* Make your own full-length book: You could crowdsource the funding to make this financially possible. Print the book through any of the online companies, or make it available online only—a less expensive way to go.

* Organize a poetry event: Get a teacher on board and host it during or at the end of a school day. Or inquire at a café in your town. Some restaurants would welcome such an event, as they'd make money from the food and drink sold to your guests.

* Create a poetry collective to publish members' books. Everybody puts in an agreed amount of money to cover the printing costs of the first publication. When it comes out, collective members get paid back some of their investment through sales, and the rest goes to publish the next person's title. This way, you can also

help each other publicize and promote your group's books.

Do keep in mind that if you publish these poems on a blog or on Twitter or in most any other way and then wish to submit that work to literary journals they'll consider these poems previously published. Many journals publish only unpublished material. You might make some of your work publicly available and keep other pieces to submit to magazines.

147

Most importantly, this is your art form, so devise ways to share your work that fit who you are. Think outside the book.

63   *Creating a Poetry Manuscript*

When you have about fifteen to twenty polished poems, you may want to put together a poetry chapbook manuscript. A chapbook is a small collection of poems. The term "chapbook" comes from a time when novels were sometimes published in newspapers one *chapter* at a time. There are many legit competitions for these small books. Beyond that, if you have about fifty poems that are ready for the world, consider putting together a complete manuscript (again, keeping in mind that even if you self-publish, literary journals will consider the poems previously published).

Deciding how to organize a book is a lot of work, but it's hardly drudgery. You get to look at all the poems you've written that you think are ready for the world and search for a through line that connects them, even obliquely. Reading lots of poetry books to see how other poets chose to order their work will be quite valuable. Some poets divide their books into thematic or chronological sections. Sometimes these sections are titled; other times, they're numbered. The book will need a title, so you have to find what ties the work together. I had the title for my most recent book of poems, *The Knot Untied*, long before I had written many of its poems.

The Knot Untied is divided into five sections that all fit under its title: "An Interlacing"—poems of connection; "Tangle"—poems a bit more complicated and difficult; "My Gordian Knot"—more complication, greater sorrow; the fourth section—"The Tie That Binds"—shows the good side of being knotted together, and includes several love poems. The last section—"The Knot Untied"— brings the book's themes together.

Another example is my anthology of poetry, *Ink Knows No Borders: Poems of the Immigrant and Refugee Experience*. The book is in a single section, allowing one poem to easily lead into the next. The reader can walk through the book without encountering any firm borders.

Decisions about the order of poems and whether to divide the book into sections require a lot of unrushed thinking through. Try out an order and ask a couple of knowledgeable people what they think.

64   *The Cover Letter*

When sending work to potential publishers, you'll need
to include a cover letter. (Plenty of sample letters may
be found online.) Tell the editor why you want to be
published in their journal and, if you've been published
before, let them know where. If it's a manuscript you're
submitting, the same considerations apply. You might
say something about why you write and why you think
they're the perfect publisher for your work. I keep query
letters simple, friendly, but to the point. Be sure all
pertinent contact information is included.

65   *Book Publishing for Poets*

Before you delve into this nuts-and-bolts chapter, take
a long, cool drink of water and be sure you're ready for
something unlike what you've read in this book so far.
This is important information but it may cause some
people to flinch because it's the antithesis of trusting
your imagination and writing with enlivened surprise!

After getting a lot of publishing credits from well-re-
spected journals under your belt, book publishers may
be interested in publishing your first book. Having many
poems published in highly regarded journals tells book
publishers that you're the real deal. Collections of poems
don't tend to be best sellers (unless you're Rupi Kaur),
but your publishing history means that your work has

been successfully vetted and that your poems are being read, two compelling reasons for a publisher to take a risk on your book. A publisher also wants to know you're going to work to get your new book into buyers' hands—that you'll give readings to promote it.

Publishing a book is costly. A publisher invests seriously in creating books—in salaries, printing, publicity, etc.—and wants to be as assured as possible that they're not going to lose a lot of money on your book. In book publishing, as in any business, people need to make money in order to be successful, but also just to survive. And success for you, the poet, means having your book favorably reviewed and selling well. If that happens, the publisher will likely want your next book.

Usually, a contract is negotiated between the poet or their agent and the publishing house. The contract states the terms of the agreement between poet and publisher, and their respective obligations to each other.

Typically, for a paperback book, the author will receive 7.5 percent of the cover price in royalties. When a book sells on Amazon for less than the retail price (as it will), the author will receive a percentage of that price; the amount will depend on the arrangement the publisher has with Amazon. If the poet has an agent, the agent will receive 15 percent of the poet's percentage. There may be an advance against royalties—money that gets paid to the writer upon signing the contract. That amount is based on the writer's percentage of the minimum number of copies the publisher thinks will sell. Once the author's percentage of the book's earnings surpasses the amount they were paid upon signing the contract, the poet will then receive royalties from book sales. Because poetry collections tend not to sell a lot of copies, often no advance is paid. In this case, the poet should begin to receive royalties as soon as copies of the book begin to sell. Royalties are generally paid twice yearly. Even if there is no money coming to the author, they should receive a statement that shows how many books have sold.

Let's note right here and right now that you're probably not going to make your first million off of publishing poetry! I'm sorry to have to be the one to tell you, but maybe you knew this already so it doesn't come as a shock.

In addition to publishing a book this way, there are poetry book publishing competitions. To enter, an applicant pays a reading fee of around $20 to $50 up front (no small change) for the publisher to consider a poetry manuscript of about fifty poems. Usually, each manuscript is read by a preliminary judge. If a couple of hundred poets submit, that raises the money to pay for a famous poet to serve as the contest's final judge, to pay the publisher, and to cover the costs of printing the book. You can invest a lot of money and never win one of these, or you can invest a little and win. It's a bit of a crapshoot. I tried this method a few times, enough to decide it wasn't for me.

If your poems are strong and speak to the judges, if they're about subjects that are in vogue and are written in a style that's got traction at the moment, it's less of a crapshoot, but luck is still involved.

Then there's who you know or who someone close to you knows. If you choose to go to college and focus on poetry writing, you'll meet professors with influence. If you know poetry people—other writers, teachers, editors—and have connections with them and if they respect your work, they may be able to assist you in getting support to publish your poetry.

66 *The Poet's Perils: Rejection*

At least some of those whom you want to say yes to your poems *will* say no. This online journal or that magazine, this reading series or that slam, may not accept the poems you've given your all to—poems you may love like crazy. Rejection is as much a part of the writing process as commas and periods.

Words like "failure" or "you suck at this" or even that smallest "no" can sting. If we are labeled in ways that don't support the authenticity of who we are, we can choose to live under those labels. Or not. Hold on to the power to define who you are, and never give it away.

Rejection will make you sad, and only those with the thickest of skins will be undeterred by it. But the thinness of your skin isn't necessarily a bad thing. The thin-skinned among us are often the most empathic ones. Being tender will bring poems to you.

If an email appears in your inbox that says, "Thanks for the chance to consider your work!" (complete with an erroneous exclamation point) and goes on to say, "We're sorry but it's not what we're looking for at this time," it can be useful. If such notes can help you to hone your craft, that's a good thing. However, if you allow rejection to determine and define you, it's unlikely you'll last long as a writer.

Learn to make a separation between your poem being rejected and your entire self being dumped. Sure, you're deeply connected to your poems, but you are *not* them. Can you let the satisfaction of writing and the joy of being propelled into the next line and the next, and the feeling of having something to say, be more valuable than any negativity?

153

After a rejection, look over the poems to see if the editor was right, or partially right, or if, perhaps, you didn't do your homework before sending that particular batch of poems to that particular journal. Maybe that magazine only publishes poetry about nature and you sent some poems about the workings of machines. Or maybe the editor was having a bad day.

Some poets say that anytime we get rejected, the best medicine is to send those poems out again right away. If you do this a few times, and they continue to come back to you, look again and ask a friend or a mentor for feedback. How thick is your skin now?

67 *Living the Poet's Life*

Very few poets in the United States, if any, make a living from publishing their poems. Poetry is a form that doesn't sell as well as, say, romance novels or crime fiction. Most poets support themselves through other kinds of work. Some choose to work at jobs unrelated to writing and poetry, while others teach or work in publishing. For example, Dana Gioia, a recent poet laureate of California and former chairman of the National Endowment for the Arts, worked for General Foods Corporation until he could support himself through his writing and writing-related work. Though the amounts vary, many poets earn money related to their poetry through speaking engagements and workshops.

154   A good friend of mine is one of the most dedicated poets I know; he works hard at his craft, but he makes a living as a chiropractor. Another friend, a haiku poet, gives his homemade books away and supports himself very well as a highly accomplished jeweler.

"Unlikely" has never stopped me from anything, and I don't wish it to stop you. It's simply important to know these realities, so that you don't feel like a failure if, after devoting yourself to your craft for some years and even successfully publishing, you still make little money from poetry itself.

Shortly out of high school, I began teaching poetry to young people, some barely younger than I was. No school trained me to do this; I learned by teaching. I did earn a bachelor's degree, but not till I was in my mid-twenties.

Earning money has been a pieced-together endeavor—from working in bookstores to performing one-woman shows. Mostly, I've paid the bills and made a life through teaching poetry in schools, community and women's centers, homeless shelters, public libraries, colleges and universities, and for cancer survivors. As the editor of many poetry anthologies, I've made some money, but more importantly I've made books that have really mattered to me and others. Some of my books have brought me royalties. I write a monthly column for my local newspaper and publish articles occasionally. At one point, a friend and I started a small press—she invested the money and I did the work; I earned some money from the books we published. Basically, anywhere I'm invited and paid to teach, there I go. Nowadays, I earn most of my living by leading various workshops in public schools, a university, and in classes I offer privately.

My middle-class life has been made possible by my husband, who has earned more money than me every year we've been together. However, for the many years before he came along, I did well enough. There was always a bouquet of flowers in my living room, and I never went hungry. But I wasn't close to being financially secure. As a self-employed person, I never know for sure what work I'll have more than a few months (at best) in advance.

Should the path of the poet be how you wish to live, you will find your way. Determination and creativity are mighty powerful forces.

68 *Your Poetic License*

To work as a doctor, a license to practice medicine is needed. So it is for many professions. There's a lot of schooling, likely a bunch of tests, and if you pass you receive a license indicating that you're authorized to do that job or perform that task. To be a poet, there is no test. (Though life will test you plenty.) Nobody's permission or blessing is needed (or, for some of us, wanted). You need only write.

But in case you ever do need it, here is your very own poetic license to copy. If you share something you've written and are told by an unkind person in love with the status quo, "Hey, you can't say that!," pull your license from your wallet, throw it down on the table, and say, "Oh, yes, I can, and here's my license!"

156

POETIC LICENSE

The bearer of this license is hereby authorized
to use words in order to dive within
and discover the world.

WARNING!
Failure to employ these powers
may enrage the Muse.
Signed,
Patrice Vecchione
Muse Representative

DATE OF EXPIRATION: **Never**

---

69   *How Writing a Poem Is Like Building a Fire*

It's early spring where I live along the Central California coast, chilly enough for early morning fires in the fireplace. I get up hours before the sun does, at an hour some call night, about 4:00 a.m. I like darkness with a promise of light.

To build a fire, you start off with old news, torn bits of paper, what others may think of as garbage—the waxed paper wrapper from yesterday's cheese sandwich. Loosely ball this paper up and lay it down on the grate. On top of that, add twigs or small wood scraps—the smallest pieces go closest to the bottom. Then comes the striking of the match—the moment of alchemy—when the burning paper ignites the twigs in your hearth. Next come larger and larger logs. You can cook dinner over that fire or you can sidle up to it to get warm.

That's what writing a poem is: you begin with news and scraps of experience, what others ignore—not only the wrapper from yesterday's sandwich but snippets of conversation, memories of who you sat next to when you ate that sandwich and how warm he made you feel, the speed at which you ran laps, the feeling of your wrong answer to a question hanging in the air. You add twig words, strike the match to the page, and light it up with imagination's fuel, creating another alchemy—your way of getting the chill out and feeding yourself creatively and spiritually.

When he was ninety years old, the cellist Pablo Casals was asked why he continued to practice. "Because I think I'm making progress," Casals replied. Each time you write, you are making progress in your understanding of poetry and becoming more adept at your craft; over time, more depth will come to your work, as will a greater ease.

Beyond any other reason, write poems because you are

157

engaged and curious, because you love the surprising
leaps of imagination, because you have things to say, and
because the act of writing poems changes you—there's
that joy again when you unfold the piece of paper with
your new poem on it, read it, find yourself and part of
the world in those phrases, slip it back into the pocket of
your jeans, and smile because you realize nothing's the
same as it was before. The hearth's fire is inside you now.

PART V

Where to Go From Here:
Poetry Resources

School, university, and public libraries are excellent places to find poetry and information about it—from writing poems to finding communities of likeminded poets—and librarians are very helpful. They will probably have ideas about local poetry contests, slams, readings, festivals, other events, and literary magazines.

Below are a few poetry resource websites followed by a bibliography.

Websites where you'll find poems, essays, recommended reading lists, interviws, audio, video, and more

* **Divedapper** is a project created by the poet Kaveh Akbar that features interviews with major voices in today's poetry: https://www.divedapper.com.

* **LitHub** links to other articles on the web and offers a weekly newsletter: https://lithub.com/.

* **Poets.org** offers a wide selection of poems, essays, recommended reading lists, anthologies, interviews, and various kinds of advice: https://poets.org/ poetry-teens/.

* **Poets & Writers** is a large nonprofit organization serving creative writers. They publish the magazine *Poets & Writers*, which lists upcoming publishing opportunities and deadlines for writing contests, information that can also be found on their website: https://www.pw.org/.

* **The Poetry Foundation** offers lots of articles on

various aspects of poetry, as well as audio lectures and informal conversations and readings: https://www.poetryfoundation.org/learn/teens/.

* **Poetry Society of America** is the oldest poetry organization in the US. You'll find articles, poems, and information on upcoming events. Best of all, it's got a large database of literary organizations: https://www.poetrysociety.org/.

* **Read, Write, Think**, the website of the National Teachers of English, is directed toward teachers, but don't let that keep you away: https://www.readwritethink.org/.

* **Readpoetry.com** presents readings of poetry, interviews with poets, and creative poetry videos: https://www.readpoetry.com/.

* **Split This Rock** is an organization whose mission is to foster a national network of socially engaged poets: https://www.splitthisrock.org/.

* ***Teen Ink*** publishes poems written by teens online and in a print magazine, with opportunities to submit your own poetry, as well as information on contests, summer programs, and recommended colleges for young writers: https://www.teenink.com/poetry/.

ONLINE POETRY WORKSHOPS AND CLASSES

* The *Adroit Journal* has a free summer mentorship program for ninth- through twelfth-grade students: https://theadroitjournal.org/about/mentorship/.

* **EdX**, affiliated with Boston University, offers classes on the writing and study of poetry. Their fees are reasonable: https://www.edx.org/learn/writing/.

* **Poetry School**, out of the UK, has a range of online classes on both the writing and the study of poetry: https://poetryschool.com/.

PUBLISHING OPPORTUNITIES

* **Writing Shed** is an app by Keith Lander that offers easy-to-follow ways to organize your poems, keep notes, and manage submissions. Users have found the outlining resources to be helpful.

* **Bennington College Young Writers Award** for tenth- through twelfth-grade students: https://www.bennington.edu/events/young-writers-awards/.

* **The *Kenyon Review* Patricia Grodd Poetry Prize for Young Writers** is an annual competition: https://www.kenyonreview.org/contests/patricia-grodd/.

* **Leonard L. Milberg '53 High School Poetry Prize, Princeton University**, is awarded to eleventh-grade student writers in the US or abroad: https://arts.princeton.edu/about/opportunities/high-school-contests/poetry-contest/.

164

* *Palette Poetry* offers publishing opportunities through their various contests: https://www.palettepoetry.com/.

* *POETRY Magazine* was founded in 1912, making it the oldest monthly poetry magazine publishing work in the English language. They include work by today's best-known poets but are mostly committed to publishing work by new poets.

* **Scholastic Art & Writing Awards** have been around since 1923 and recognize teen writers and artists with vision, ingenuity, and talent through several competitions: https://www.artandwriting.org/what-we-do/the-awards/how-to-enter/.

* **Submittable** publishes a weekly newsletter with links to articles and publishing opportunities. Many small press publishers, literary journals, and contests list their upcoming information on this site. Writers can open an account at no charge and submit work through this platform: https://www.submittable.com/.

* *Teen Ink* has a number of poetry contests: https://www.teenink.com/contests/.

SPECIFIC INTEREST SITES AND ORGANIZATIONS

* **Cave Canem Foundation** is an online home for African American poetry. Cave Canem is "committed to cultivating the artistic and professional growth of African American poets": https://cavecanempoets.org/.

* **Kundiman** is an organization "dedicated to nurturing generations of writers and readers of Asian American Literature": http://www.kundiman.org/.

* **The Lambda Literary Foundation** has fostered and advocated for LGBTQ writers since 1987. They offer a writing retreat for emerging LGBTQ writers. On their site you'll find book reviews, interviews, publishing opportunities, and more: https://www.lambdaliterary.org/.

* **The Women's National Book Association** "was established in 1917, before women in America had the right to vote": https://wnba-books.org/.

* **#undocupoets** promotes work by undocumented poets. Their mission is to "raise consciousness about the structural barriers" that undocumented poets face: https://twitter.com/hashtag/undocupoets.

ANNOTATED BIBLIOGRAPHY

Here's a list of other books to support your work.

Addonizio, Kim. *Ordinary Genius: A Guide for the Poet Within*. **New York: W. W. Norton, 2009.**
Addonizio shares her own writing process and encourages writers to find inspiration in poetry recent and old.

Hacker, Marilyn, Kazim Ali, Donald Hall, Annie Finch, David Lehman, eds. *Poets on Poetry*. **123 vols. Ann Arbor: University of Michigan Press, 1978–2019.**
Some recent books in the series are *Resident Alien: On Border-crossing and the Undocumented Divine* by Kazim Ali, *Pivotal Voices, Era of Transition: Toward a 21st Century Poetics* by Rigoberto González, *The Mirror Diary: Selected Essays* by Garrett Hongo, and *Noise that Stays Noise: Essays* by Cole Swenson. These books are terrific but they're a bit pricey. Check with your public library to see if interlibrary loans are offered.

Heilbrun, Carolyn G. *Writing a Woman's Life*. **New York: W. W. Norton, 1988.**
A case for women to write the complicated truths about their lives.

Hoagland, Tony. *The Art of Voice: Poetic Principles and Practice*. **New York: W. W. Norton, 2019.**
This is the best book on poetic voice I've read—it's clear, accessible, and chock-full of writing prompts.

Kuusisto, Stephen, Deborah Tall, and David Weiss,

eds. *The Poet's Notebook: Excerpts from the Notebooks of 26 American Poets.* **New York: W. W. Norton, 1995.**
This is a collection of journal entries from such poets as Donald Hall, Joy Harjo, Yusef Komunyakaa, Mary Oliver, and Charles Simic. Each selection is preceded by comments about the journal by their author, and some are followed by a poem.

167

Rilke, Rainer Maria. *Letters to a Young Poet.* **Translated by Stephen Mitchell. New York: Vintage Books, 1984.**
A timeless collection of advice to an emerging poet. "[O]nly be attentive to what is arising within you, and place that above everything that you perceive around you. What is happening in your innermost being is worthy of your whole love."

Ueland, Brenda. *If You Want to Write: A Book About Art, Independence and Spirit.* **New York: G. P. Putnam's Sons, 1938.**
First published in 1938, this book continues to be in print because it's both reliable and encouraging, especially to new writers. Read it for a reminder of the value of your own voice and creative spirit. *If You Want to Write* is published by more than one house and is easy to find.

Vecchione, Patrice. *Step into Nature: Nurturing Imagination and Spirit in Everyday Life.* **New York: Atria Books/Beyond Words, 2015**.
Join me for walk in nature to enliven your creativity and express yourself through various forms.

Acknowledgments

When I needed a reader, Cheryl Joseph, longtime friend and English teacher, was right there, with her beautiful "yes!" She read draft after draft with great care, smarts, and understanding, making this book much better than it would have been without her. Cristin De Vine helped explain me to myself, and I'm forever grateful. My best beloved, Michael Stark, offered his patience, tenderness, and love, as he always does. More students than I can count, from preschoolers through those much older than that, have brought their wonder and depth to my classes, and each of them helped write these pages. Early, life-altering support came from Roberta Bristol, Julie Olsen Edwards, Don Rothman, Gael Roziere, and Gina Van Horn. I'm thankful to Charlotte Raymond, for her enthusiasm for my work, saying, "You're meant to write this book!"; to Dan Simon, first for *Ink Knows No Borders*, and now for *My Shouting, Shattered, Whispering Voice*, for believing in the voices—shouting or otherwise—of young people and for believing in mine; to Lauren Hooker, oh, Queen of Repetition Prevention, for your care and kindness; Ruth Weiner, you make things happen, and with grace. Kim Addonizio, Marcelo Hernandez Castillo, Safia Elhillo, and Sara Michas-Martin generously responded to my questions about poetry and writing process. Fred Courtright, King of Permissions, you made all the difference. For smoothing the rough spots, thank you to Rosie King, Sara Michas-Martin, and Elliot Ruchowitz-Roberts. Two small, loud-purring beings, Ace and Stella, accompany me daily; I'd be remiss to not thank them here.

Permissions